ON REFLECTION

Touch and Go

Margaret R. Forrester

SAINT ANDREW PRESS

First published in 2002 by
SAINT ANDREW PRESS
121 George Street
Edinburgh EH2 4YN

Copyright © Margaret R. Forrester, 2002

ISBN 0 7152 0800 4

British Library Cataloguing in Publication Data
A catalogue record for this book is available from the British Library

Typeset by Waverley Typesetters, Galashiels
Printed and bound by Creative Print & Design, Wales

Contents

Touching the World – through Politics

Keeping in Touch – with the Church

A Touching Place – Jesus

Preface

For most of my life, from childhood onwards, sermons have bored me. Occasionally there would be one that was different. It may have filled my eyes with tears or enflamed my heart. The best of them would open the Bible in such a way that the people and the events became real. I was invited or commanded to think, to decide, to take God seriously. As Job said, 'I had heard of you by the hearing of the ear, but now my eye sees you; therefore . . . I repent in dust and ashes.' [1]

Because of this, all my preaching life, I have tried to open the Bible in ways that were honest and straightforward, easily remembered and challenging. Nearly always I have used a lectionary, so that with the congregation, we explore a wide range of readings and biblical themes. With length of years have come shorter and simpler sermons. Even so, they are sometimes boring, even to me!

In 1999, for two months, I had the surprising joy of being the Roach Trust exchange preacher in Toorak Uniting Church, Melbourne, Australia. I am indebted to the warm and welcoming hospitality of that generous congregation, and especially because they first encouraged me to write this book.

However, for over twenty years the congregation of St Michael's, Edinburgh, has listened patiently to my sermons. If I have learned anything about preaching I owe it to their kindly criticism and encouragement, both of which are largely silent, and therefore must be listened to the more carefully.

So to Toorak Uniting Church, Melbourne, but supremely and specially to St Michael's, Edinburgh, this book of sermons is gratefully and affectionately dedicated.

MARGARET R. FORRESTER

NOTE

1. Job 42:5, 6.

In Touch – with Heaven

Can't Stop Loving

E-MAIL FROM JOHN

Readings:	Acts 8:26–40
	1 John 4:7–21
	John 15:1–10
Season:	Fifth Sunday of Easter

People who are used to computers and e-mail and surfing the net, know a great deal more than I do. I am still fairly nervous and press buttons and hope that I am doing the right thing. When I was preparing this service, and thinking about John who wrote about the vine, John who wrote about loving each other, I must have pressed a very powerful button indeed because I received an e-mail straight from heaven, specially for us.

To:
saintsalive@stmichaels.co.edinburgh.scotland

From:
john@patronsaints.cloudnine.seventhheaven.co.eternity

As I read it, I remembered that John was said to be a bit younger than the other apostles. He may have been the brother of James, fisher folk, like Peter and Andrew. They were known as the Sons of Thunder – so someone in the family made a lot of noise, and he wrote of himself in the gospel, as the one whom Jesus loved.

So he was a beloved and loving person. There is a legend that, unlike many of the apostles, he was not a martyr, but lived to a great age and died peacefully. This is the text of the e-mail, a message from John, straight to us!

From John the Evangelist, to my brothers and sisters in Christ, grace and peace in the name of the Lord Jesus.

I am glad that you have read again the words I wrote so long ago about the gardener and the vine. I often think about it even now. Heaven is perfection, but life on earth had a quality of adventure about it that was exciting and mysterious and dangerous. That particular day, we had been walking on the hills around Jerusalem and passed a farm where an old man was tending his vines. We watched his gnarled hands, tough and hardy, with hard ribbed nails, and veins standing out like ropes. Yet they were as sensitive as a young girl's, running along the branches, stripping off the old dead bark and cutting back to the new shoots, which were fruiting spurs. How well he knew the plants, and how carefully and lovingly he tended them, almost as if they were children.

Jesus stopped, we all did for we were ready for a rest, and we passed the time of day. The old man and his wife brought out some bread and wine and olives, and we shared them together in the sunshine. Jesus asked questions about growing grapes and harvesting them and making wine. I thought he was just being polite, but he was really interested. We learned how deep the roots go, how carefully the farmer dresses them with manure and compost, and how carefully they have to be cleaned and stripped each year, otherwise there is no crop.

Then, we said our thanks to that lovely old couple and moved on. We followers were eager to start talking again about the coming of the Kingdom. About when, and how, Jesus would enter Jerusalem in triumph. But Jesus said, 'No. No. No.' Then he paused and said, 'Listen. I am the vine.' We thought he was wandering a bit. Maybe he had a touch of the sun? We had been talking about the Kingdom. The Kingdom – and there he was blethering about gardening! 'Listen. I am the vine. And my father, God, is the gardener, the farmer. You are the branches. So you must stick to me just as I stay close to my Father. That way there will be lots of fruit and we shall have a good harvest.'

He kept on saying that we must stay close to him. 'Abide in me. And I in you. Together we shall have lots of fruit. But we must stay close together.'

The week that he died he spoke about it again to remind us, so it became fixed in my mind. The vine is Jesus. The gardener is God. And we, all the disciples, whether you in Edinburgh or us in Palestine, we are the branches. So we belong to Jesus. I found it a funny sort of picture, but he was very insistent that we remember it. Then, later on, he spoke about not staying close, but about going out. 'As the Father sent me, I send you.'

How can we stay attached to him and at the same time go out and tell people? It worried me a lot. I was able to understand why we had to stay close to him – otherwise we would forget. Besides, we were strong when we were with him. But going out into all the world was scary. It was so lonely without him. I would have gone to the ends of the earth *with* him. We all would. But alone? We were frightened.

It wasn't until long after the terrible Friday when he died and the strange time of coming and going, which we call the resurrection, that gradually we began to see what he might have meant. And the key word in it all is Love.

God sent him to show all of us what love is. Jesus spent all his time and energy and power in showing us that love of God in action. His love was so powerful that he could stretch out his hand and someone who was sick became better. It was astonishing.

I have seen people who were blind able to see, and folk with mental illness become well. More than that, I have seen ordinary folk stressed out of their wits and worried to death able to relax within his love. But it cost Jesus a lot. He was always exhausted afterwards, as though some life force had drained out of him, as though the love he had from God passed out in the healing.

Gradually I began to see that he was Life and Light. He was Living Water and True Bread. He was Breath and Spirit. In him was fullness of living. He was Love Incarnate.

His attitude to us was always one of love. From time to time we would have a bit of a spat, or even an outright argument. People do get scratchy with each other. Jesus always knew what was going on and made us sort it out before we went any further. He never seemed to lose his temper, although you could see that sometimes he would be shattered with tiredness. So everything he said or did was to teach us about love.

Our unwillingness, or inability, to understand God's love and the love Jesus had were what brought him to that awful cross. I still weep over that Friday. Even in heaven I weep. And yet in a strange way I glory in it, too. He loved us so much that he was willing to do *that* for us. Was it not only for us, but also for Judas and Pilate, for Herod and Caiaphas and all those wicked people who put him there? Perhaps it was especially for them. Even in heaven I marvel at the depth of the divine love.

So when he says 'Abide in me,' I think he means that whatever happens we must let God's love be in us. We must learn to let our resentments go, and our anger, and our prejudices, and our ambition, and the little angry thoughts that are in our heads, and let the love of God fill us to the brim. And *then* we go out to share the love of God with other people, to tell them of the love of Jesus, to tell them of the cross and the resurrection, to tell them of forgiveness and new starts and the peace that can flood your soul.

We disciples did try, we really did try, to live in love. And as we tried, we found that we were able to spread the news and to share the love of God. Peter turned out to be amazingly brave. He could think on his feet and talk fast, could Peter. I always liked to think through things and reflect on them and then I wrote them down if I had the chance.

There was that time with Philip and the official from Ethiopia. God made sure they were in the right place at the right time. And because of that, a whole new Christian country was born in Africa – yes, Ethiopia in Africa was Christian long before you folk in Scotland heard about Jesus!

My dear friends in Edinburgh, remember the love of God. Let it beat in your hearts and course in your veins. If, at home or work or church, tempers are frayed, or worry predominates, or apathy sets in, stop what you are doing and remember the love of God, which surrounds you and holds you up. If you want to blame someone else or have the glory for yourself or feel you are the only one doing the work, remember the love of God, which bled for you and died for you and lives for you.

Abide in him. For he is the true vine. Go into the world and share that love. But always come back for more. You need to return again and again. Let his love keep you living and loving.

My little children, let the love of God lead you. Farewell. The grace of the Lord Jesus Christ be with you, the saints of Edinburgh in St Michael's.

2

Not from Nothing!

CORRESPONDENCE BETWEEN
ANDREW AND PHILIP

Readings:	*Ephesians 3:14–21*
	John 6:1–15
Season:	*Seventh Sunday after Pentecost*

The gospel reading is the story of the feeding of the multitudes
with the bread and the fish. It is a story so well known it is almost
insulting to go over it again. But there is always something fresh
there, especially taken with the reading from the Ephesians. I am
taking the liberty of imagining that the two disciples who were
named and active in the story, Philip and Andrew, are writing to
each other many years later.

Philip writes first.

My dear Andrew,

Grace to you and peace in the Lord Jesus Christ. The Christian
congregation here sends greetings. Some of the people here are
anxious that I may die or be executed before our dear Lord returns,
and they have been at me to tell them some more of his teachings
and to describe some of the things that he did. Yesterday, I told
them about the time we had the food crisis. Do you remember
that?

There were hordes of people there. I mean there were *crowds* – like a pop concert of sorts. I could see them coming and I pulled at his sleeve. 'Send them away,' I whispered to him. 'Send them away.' I could see that there would be problems. All these people with their insatiable demands on his time and his energy. And then Jesus turns to me as bold as brass with that funny little smile he had, 'Now, where are we going to get enough food for these folk, Philip?'

'Gracious,' I replied. 'We can't do that! It would take a fortune to buy food for them. And we don't carry that sort of money. There's going to be trouble. Send them away, Jesus, for God's sake, send them away.'

'For God's sake . . .' he said. 'For *God*'s sake, Philip? Oh, I don't think so.' And I swear he winked at me!

I've thought about it so often and I was trying to explain to the people at our own fellowship here that it wasn't a piece of magic. It wasn't just an amazing miracle – although of course it was. It was more like a miracle and an acted sermon all in one.

First, Jesus didn't conjure the food for everyone out of thin air. It wasn't just something out of nothing. He obviously wanted us to participate. I have often wondered since if he could have turned stones into bread. Could he really have fed us all with nothing in his hands? And the more I think about it, the more I feel he really had to have something from us first. It wasn't bread from nothing. It wasn't food from the air. It was food for all because we put something into his hands – at least that wee boy did. Do you remember the grin on his face when Jesus was so pleased? I'm told he is one of the leaders of the church in Tiberias now. So the really important thing is that we should continue to offer to Jesus even things that we feel are not very good or not enough or too simple or not clever enough. If we offer them to Jesus, he will use what we give. More than that, if we do *not* offer what we have, maybe, just maybe, he can do nothing. Think of that – Jesus can do nothing without us.

The second thing I feel about that incident was the way Jesus expected us to take responsibility for that crowd. They were nothing to do with us. They weren't committed to him the way we were. They just . . . well . . . I don't know why they came. But Jesus took them so seriously and expected us to as well. Even after they had had their fill most of them went home again and never gave it a second thought. Some of us became angry. 'They're just using you, Jesus, just *using* you.'

'Yes,' he agreed, and looked quite happy.

But I've been thinking recently that perhaps Jesus was trying to tell us something. Maybe the great crowd out there that Jesus tried to help is our responsibility.

I get such satisfaction and joy from worshipping in our church fellowship – we all know Jesus and love him. But when I walk to church past those bullying Roman guards and the crowds in the market place and all the riffraff that is around, I wonder. Was Jesus telling us that we should be out there doing something for them? Like feeding them or telling them about God's love. I tell you it really worries me. But I feel now that what Jesus was really saying, when he asked me to feed them, was this, 'All of you have a responsibility to look after people. No selfish, "me first" attitudes. All of you must take responsibility for everyone.'

The third thing was to do with the simplest offerings. Frankly, if that child had come to me with his fish and rolls I would have told him not to be silly. Stupid squashed barley bread and two dried fish! Who did he think he was, bothering the Master like that? And then Jesus took those squashed sandwiches and . . . heaven opened before us. I mean . . . it wasn't good enough for me, but it was more than enough for Jesus.

Sometimes, Andrew, I worry that even in the Christian church we are obsessed with the grand and the imposing and the wealthy. We have one very wealthy member in our own congregation and it is easy to treat him with respect simply because he pays for so much. But Jesus wasn't like that. I must try harder to value the little things that people can do, and to appreciate the gifts of children, poor folk, simple people, well-meaning people. Jesus took that simple offering so seriously.

Anyway, my dear Andrew, these are my thoughts:

1. Jesus didn't conjure the food for everyone out of thin air; he needed us.
2. Jesus expected us to take responsibility for that crowd, and still does today.
3. Jesus accepted the simplest offerings, and so should we.

Do write back if you have the chance. God bless you and your congregation.

And here is part of the letter that Andrew wrote back.

My very dear Philip,

What a wonderful letter! It took me back to that hillside as though it were yesterday. What panic we were in and how calm he was. Oh yes, there was more to that picnic than meets the eye. The barley bread was not the only bread. The food for our stomachs was not the only food. The child was wiser than the adults. And that *glaikit*[1] mob knew where to find living bread. And what about the twelve of us, bent double picking up the pieces. What was that all about? I'm still wondering. I sometimes think Jesus was poking fun at us.

I am glad your church is going over the story. When we break bread each Lord's Day we often remember it too. I like your three points:

Jesus needed us.

Jesus gives us responsibility for the mob outside.

Jesus accepted the simplest offerings, and so should we.

For me, the most important lesson is that God is able to accomplish abundantly far more than all we can ask or imagine. God's love is so enormous.

- It holds us when we are breaking.
- It comforts us in sorrow.
- It is not soft or sloppy.
- It sometimes hurts because more is demanded of us.
- It is strong enough to take with us to the lions.
- It is always there with purpose and power and direction.

And that love, when it works through us, can do astonishing things. Not by waving a magic wand, but by using our sweat and toil and prayers. None of us could possibly have imagined that feeding. We might have left it all to God, and then nothing would have happened. It had to be that way – our stupidity, the wee boy's generosity, the patience of Jesus and the hunger of the crowds. And there was food for everyone, more than we could ask, more than we could imagine. The love of God is able still to accomplish unimaginable things. But we have to get stuck in.

My very dear Philip, thank you for sharing. May God's abundant love be with you and your congregation. God's grace be with you all.

NOTE

1. *glaikit*: foolish, stupid, of low intelligence, thoughtless, irresponsible (*The Concise Scots Dictionary*).

3

The Trouble with Foreigners

E-MAIL FROM PETER[1]

Readings:	*Acts 10:44–8*
	John 15:9–17
Season:	*Sixth Sunday of Easter*

I've had another amazing e-mail straight from heaven! This time it comes from Peter. What a pompous ass he was to begin with. But he could take a joke against himself quite well. Judge for yourself. Here is his e-mail instead of a sermon.

To:
saintsalive@stjohnevangelist.co.edinburgh.scotland

From:
simonpeter@patronsaints.cloudnine.seventhheaven.co.eternity

Grace to you and peace in the Lord Jesus Christ. I was delighted to know that on Sunday you will be reading and thinking of that time when I was so stupid and stubborn about foreigners and gentiles. The words that Luke wrote in that long piece to Theophilus, what you call the book of Acts, are not enough to explain what really happened. He was too kind to me by half, so I thought I would fill you in with some details.

It was like this. I had been taking part in an evangelistic tour around the coast with some degree of success. Saul's conversion made a great difference to us and we were able to go forward spreading the gospel – to the Jews of course, which seemed right and proper. After a very busy time, I lodged with a man who was also called Simon at the beautiful port of Jaffa, next to the great new city that you call Tel Aviv.

The house overlooked the port, where there were craft from all over the world. I was famished. The meal was not yet ready so I went up to the rooftop to pray and give thanks. There was a breeze from the sea which made the high temperatures bearable but it was still hot. What with the heat, and my hunger, and the smells of cooking food wafting up, and the sails from all the nations dancing in the sun, I dropped off into a deep sleep. And while I slept, I had a dream.

A great sheet or sail, just like the sails in the harbour, was let down from heaven with all sorts of animals – and I mean all sorts, deer, pig, shellfish, things that are forbidden – and a voice from heaven said, 'Rise, Peter, rise and eat.' I know temptation when I see it. 'Not at all,' I said. 'I'm not that desperate, I can wait.' But I *was* hungry. Then the voice came again. 'Don't you call unclean what I have made.'

Well the same thing happened again. In my dream, I mean. By this time I was ravenous in real life *and* in my dream, and everything was smelling *so* good. 'Get up and eat, Peter,' the voice said. 'Certainly not,' I said. 'I have eaten *kosher* all my life and I shall continue to do so.' The voice came again: 'Are you calling what *I have made* unfit, or unclean, or imperfect?'

It happened a third time. By this time I was starving. And it was all I could do to refuse. A third time the voice said, 'How dare you, part of my creation, call any part of it unclean! Are you calling what I have made unfit for human consumption?' And

12

just for a minute, I thought I heard the sound of snorting laughter just like Jesus used to make when he was teasing me.

Then I woke up still with that great aroma of roast chicken stuffed with red peppers and olives in my nostrils. Actually what wakened me was a thunderous knocking on the door.

I ran downstairs and when I saw the men at the door, I stiffened. Foreigners. Gentiles. In uniform. That lot. Was it my turn now, as it had been for Stephen?

'We come from Cornelius,' they said. 'He is a God-fearing man who gives much to the Jewish cause and prays regularly himself as well as his household. He feels that God wants you to explain things to him.'

For a moment I wondered. Was it a trick? And then I realised that *this* was what the dream was about.

'Come in, come in. We are just going to eat. You must join us.' And so they came, ate (that stuffed chicken was *wonderful!*), boarded for the night and the next morning we set out to meet Cornelius in Caesarea.

All the time we travelled, I had to rearrange my thoughts. The man I was to meet was a gentile. A good gentile, but a gentile, a non-Jew. He wasn't *one of us*. So that was maybe what the dream was about. Maybe we were going to have to admit non-Jews as followers of the Way. They would have to become Jews first, of course. If that were the case we should have to arrange for circumcision and instruction for him and for his family. Then after a decent interval, perhaps a couple of years, there would be the baptism. It was unusual, but it could be done. So the meaning of the dream became clearer. We were all made by God. We were almost, up to a point, equal.

When we arrived, the whole family was there. Cornelius, a tall, imposing man bowed low. 'Stand up,' I said, with great magnanimity. 'We are both men made by God.'

When I went into the room I made it clear to them what had happened. I explained that my religion would not normally permit me to associate with them but that I believed that God was calling us to something new.

I started at the beginning. Clearly, it would take several long sermons to make the point. When suddenly the Holy Spirit fell on them, on *them* – that uncircumcised, unclean lot! I thought I heard that Jesus-laugh again, but it must have been my imagination. So I took a deep breath and called for water and made the best of a difficult situation. It was not what I had planned. It was not what I had expected. In fact, I felt as though someone was playing tricks on me.

I thought I heard that gurgle of laughter again. And I remembered Jesus looking at me with that smile in his eyes, throwing out a challenge, 'Follow me, Peter the Fisherman, and I will make you a fisherman all right. You will catch bigger fish than these!'

Bigger fish than these . . . I looked at Cornelius and it suddenly came into focus. Jesus! He always had something up his sleeve. We had the most wonderful baptism. It was great. I remembered then that Jesus had said, 'You did not choose me; I chose you.' And he chose us not by instructing us but by loving us. We had never felt so loved in our lives as when we were with him. And now Jesus had chosen Cornelius by loving him, and he had got me involved. I began to see the funny side of this. And then I really did hear the snorting Jesus-laugh! So that, my friends, is what happened.

Now *you* have to work out who are the people you know, or do not know, who do not belong. Who are the people who 'are not one of us'? The people that you think of as I, Peter, felt about Cornelius?

- Are they different denominations?

- Are they working class or upper class?

- Are they militant soldiers or weak-kneed pacifists?

- Are they from very different political parties?

- Are they in prison?

- Do they have AIDS?

- Are they homosexual or lesbian?

- Are they homeless and rootless, smug and suburban, or well-heeled and love shooting?

The chances are that Jesus has chosen them by loving them. And you must love them, too. Otherwise how will they know that Jesus has chosen them? Remember the mistake I made with Cornelius – and do better.

The grace and peace, the laughter and wisdom of the Lord Jesus Christ be with you. Amen.

NOTE

1. This sermon was preached at the church of St John the Evangelist, Princes Street, Edinburgh.

4

More than Bread

E-MAIL FROM JOHN

Readings:	*1 Kings 2:10–12, 3:3–14*
	Ephesians 5:15–20
	John 6:51–8
Season:	*Tenth Sunday after Pentecost*

I have had another e-mail from heaven. I never expect them – that would be presumptuous. And I have no idea which button on my machine produces them. But when they come I am grateful. This one came slowly, as though the person writing it was old or ill or did not want to rush into print. So perhaps we should listen to the message gently and savour it. Here is what arrived through my printer:

To:

saintsalive@stmichaels.co.edinburgh.scotland

From:

john@patronsaints.cloudnine.seventhheaven.co.eternity

My very dear friends, greetings to you. Grace and peace from the dear Lord Jesus be in your hearts and lives. Greet one another, and build your fellowship through his love and in his strength.

It gives me such joy to know that you on earth are studying the words I wrote long ago. You have been thinking about that time when Jesus fed the people. You think it happened once? You think it happened twice? My friends, it happened all the time. Constantly he said things that meant more to me than the bread I had for my supper – and I would be hungry enough in those days, being young and strong. We would all be walking along the road and he would suddenly point to a bird, or a flower, or a beggar, or a farmer, and then speak to us or tell us stories and . . . words almost fail me. Look at the flowers of the field, how they grow . . . Solomon in all his glory was not clothed like one of these. I could never see a flower after that without seeing its beauty and praising God. Once he saw a beggar at the gate of a rich businessman's house. The wealthy businessman ignored the beggar and ordered his servants to do the same. Then Jesus told us the story of the rich man and Lazarus, which Luke wrote down. I was always carefully suspicious of the use of money after that.

Oh yes, after he had left us and gone ahead of us, the whole earth looked different to me because we had been with him. We were so privileged. I'm sorry, I am rambling on.

You think we wrote down a lot, in these four accounts that you call Matthew, Mark, Luke and John? We could not remember a fraction of the teaching or the stories. I found it hard to express the certainty of love that Jesus had for his heavenly Father and the sense of love he gave to each of us. And I don't think we ever knew how much we grieved him when we argued or had a quarrel. He felt the pain of our quarrels acutely. And even now, in majesty and glory, he grieves for the pain on earth. Heaven is not painless, you know. All the unresolved griefs and agonies of your earth are held here in love and prayer and weeping – and in faith. We shall not let you down. We shall not let you go. My little children, you cannot understand, but one day you will. Please believe me when I tell you that heaven is not perfect and cannot be until you, all of you, are in perfect love and charity with one another. It's hard work in heaven praying for all of you, but we do it gladly.

My friends, I am wandering away from the point. Jesus fed people. There is no doubt about that. There was bread and there was fish. With my own eyes, I saw it. But I saw more than that. And I wanted so much for all that crowd to see the real food that Jesus had to offer. All they could see was bread unlimited and full bellies – no bad thing to see if you have ever watched a child crying with hunger or an old man starving to death. Indeed, in his name you *must* share food with the hungry. He has commanded it. But there is more to it than bread.

That is why I said and I wrote, 'See and believe.' 'See and believe.' 'See and believe.' They still saw only bread. So I want to set out for you now what was there as well as the bread and the fish.

First, *the real food is Jesus*. No, of course we don't eat him. That was a wilful misunderstanding by people who should have known better. 'How can this man give us his flesh to eat?' they asked. Misguided people! Jesus is as *necessary* to us as food. That is the point. We can exist on what goes into our mouths. But we need Jesus and the love he gives for true living.

Sometimes I see people broken by grief, or depression, or sadness, and I know, and you know, that what they need is not bread but love. That is what I meant when I wrote that Jesus gives himself as bread for the life of the world. When people are broken by grief, or depression, or sadness, it is agony for us in heaven to see their plight. For they need Jesus so badly.

Sometimes they are too proud to come for help. Sometimes they are so busy shouting for what they want that they will not let Jesus whisper a few words of comfort. Sometimes the sound of their weeping is so loud it fills up the space around them and they do not even see the hands offered in friendship – often, often, that is the way Jesus sends his love. And sometimes people have decided that there is no God – that matters less than you may think – but then the Lord has to find other ways to wrap his love around them. And when they feel the love, maybe they do not recognise it. Never mind. God is happy to wait. People who receive love and give love are not far from the Kingdom of God. Sometimes people who profess God can be hard of heart, and stern of mind, and unloving to their brothers and sisters on earth.

Whoever you are, wherever you are, you need Jesus and the love he gives for your life. That is as essential as the bread on your plate. That is the first message.

The second thing I want to say to you good folk at St Michael's is that you must stay close to Jesus. I wrote down what I believed, that Jesus was truly (but not literally) saying, 'My flesh is real food. My blood is real drink. Whoever eats my flesh and drinks my blood possesses eternal life and I will raise him up on the last day.'

It was true, of course, that his dear body was butchered for us. We saw the flesh and we saw the blood. But that was not what I meant. I want you to know that we must partake of the *essential Jesus*. We must experience the intensity of his love and the reality of his sacrifice for us. It all came together for us at his last supper. As you know, I never even wrote about the eating part of the meal. It was the message afterwards that was important to me about serving each other and loving each other, even to the extent of washing people's feet.

Let us go back to the supper. We did not know then that it would be his last meal with us, although he dropped fairly clear hints. But at the last supper he shared the bread with us – again! 'This is my body,' he said – it was clearly bread. 'This is my blood,' he said – and we could see it was a cup of wine. As we ate and drank, we had never been so close, almost as though we were part of him.

So after the death and the rising, we kept on meeting to share bread and wine, and to remember his words and to recall his presence. We knew that we had to stay close and this turned out to be the best possible way. As we ate and drank together, we felt him to be so near, so close to each of us and to all of us, he was truly present, unseen but there. It is still true.

So keep close to Jesus, break bread together and share the wine.

The third thing I want to write to you today is that *Jesus is eternal*. Jesus was brutally clear to some of these very religious people. 'The bread I give is not like the bread which our fathers ate. They ate it and died. This bread will last.' We found that difficult ourselves. Because when someone is dead, he or she is dead. Then wonderfully, Jesus was dead and also alive. He was alive as we shared bread and wine. But he was alive from the tomb, although he wasn't around all the time. But certainly he was alive.

More than that, his words were alive. His stories were alive. His truth was alive. And his love is alive and rich and warm and for ever. Jesus is for always.

Of course, my dear friends, you will know the sting of death as you lose someone you love. You will have to face death yourself. We were all frightened of dying. There was always the terror of the cross, the lions, the flames, the stones, and some of us quietly or unquietly in our own beds. Often death means weakness or pain. Yes, death is real. But Jesus who has entered death walks with you and brings you to life. Jesus is eternal.

So, my dear friends, the sting of death is real enough, but physical death is only part of the story. Please believe this. From where we are in heaven, death is such a short moment in what you call time. And yet for you it can be so long. It is in truth a short step for the spirit to take and then the fullness of God's love takes care of you and brings you into such shining eternal life and love.

But that shining eternal life and love start on earth. That is what I meant by the true bread. There, on your beautiful earth, you have union with him. There, on your God-given earth you taste eternal joy in Jesus, true bread. Truly, this is the bread which came down from heaven. Whoever eats this bread will live for ever.

My little children in St Michael's, continue to know Jesus, the true bread of heaven. Continue in love and service. Continue to love one another. The love and grace of the Lord Jesus Christ be with you all. I, John, greet you in his name.

Touching Base – in Trouble

5

The Only Problem

Readings: *Job 13:1–13*
            Job 38:1–7
            Job 42:1–6

Job is a big book to read. I think it helps if we see the whole work, not just as a story, not just as poetry, but as a play. And the thing we must be clear about is that this *is* a story. It is not history. It is not factual. It is a way of working through a mega-problem; how can we believe in a good God who allows human suffering? It has been described as 'The Only Problem'.[2]

I want you to think of this church as a theatre. We're going to have an apron stage running out into the congregation, so that we can see the action in the round. There will be a minstrels' gallery, where there will be a lot of action. And we'll have stairs coming down from the gallery to join the main chancel area.

The play opens. Centre stage is Job. 'The greatest of all the people in the East', with his wife and his seven perfect sons and his seven perfect daughters, with their spouses and their cattle, wealth unlimited and all of them praising God.

Up in the minstrels' gallery, scene one starts. God is there, with all the heavenly beings, and the accuser, or Satan.

'Where have you been?' asks God.

'I've been walking up and down, walking up and down.'

'Have you considered my servant Job?' says God. 'Isn't he wonderful! No-one like him on earth.'

'Well,' says Satan, 'no wonder! You've put a fence around him and a cushion under him. Just stretch out your hand; he'll curse you to your face.' So permission is granted, but not to harm Job himself.

Action moves to the main stage for the second scene.

With all the suddenness of a fairy tale, everything vanishes: oxen, donkeys, sheep, camels, servants, sons, daughters. They are wiped out in a night. Only Job and his wife are left. Then comes the quote that everyone knows:

> Naked I came from my mother's womb, and naked shall I return there. The Lord gave and the Lord has taken away; blessed be the name of the Lord.

Back to the gallery for the third scene.

'I *told* you that Job was a good man,' says God.

'Touch his bone and he will curse you to your face,' says Satan.

'All right,' says God. 'But you are not to kill him.'

Centre stage for the fourth scene.

Job is afflicted with sores – raging itchiness and putrid boils. And still Job did not sin. Enter the notorious three comforters. They are so appalled at Job's suffering that they sit with him in total silence for seven days and seven nights. And that was the best thing that they did. Then they begin to speak. Each of them makes a lengthy speech and Job answers each of them. Basically, they say the same type of thing.

The first one starts by saying, 'If you don't mind my saying . . .' That's a certain opening for trouble! And they say things like:

- The innocent never perish, therefore you must have sinned.
- Turn to God; he'll make it better.
- Have you tried praying about it?

And all the time, Job is in another world of pain and anguish, saying, 'I just want to die.' He says to the so-called comforters: 'Leave me alone, you voyeurs, you watchers of humanity, you people-peepers.'

The awful three persist, with their maddening half-truths and religious clichés – maddening because there is just enough in what they say to make you feel that they have something.

- God *never* rejects a blameless person.
- You probably deserve even more punishment.
- Do be quiet, Job, you're undermining religion.

And then Job turns on them with the words we read in chapter 13:

If you want to be wise; be silent!
I want to speak to God.
I want to put my case to God.

And you . . . you are arguing dishonestly for God! God doesn't need your patchwork of lies. How *dare* you argue so wickedly for God! Do you really think that you can cheat God the way you cheat another human being?

And while the three comforters chatter on with their false comfort and specious arguments, Job is climbing theological mountains. He is beginning to break out of the prison house of his faith that had become too small.

Job discovers that his suffering is not isolated. There is much suffering and injustice in the world. And he may even have been responsible for some. And he is certainly accountable for doing nothing about it.

27

And he discovers, most significantly, that God is not the quasi-magician that he had thought.

Suddenly, as though he could stand the charade and the agony no longer, God himself leans over the gallery and bursts into speech, words of breathtaking imagery and poetry from chapter 38: 'Then the Lord answered Job out of the whirlwind . . .'

God explains how loving wisdom was at the heart of creation, giving birth to the created world, putting breath and life and freedom into every living creature. God does not exist to be answerable or accountable to human beings. In a salvo of questions that are like magnificent fireworks of majesty, wisdom and justice, Job is corrected for daring to misrepresent the holiness of God and the creatureliness of humankind. God questions Job about his pretensions and his misapprehensions: 'Where were you, were you there, when I laid the foundations of the earth and all the morning stars shouted for joy?'

The poetry rolls on. God's love has created and sustains creation. God's love underpins everything. God's free love has been gifted to us.

And in the climax of the book, God leaves the minstrels' gallery, leaves the heavenly bodies, and comes to Job with open and loving arms.

And Job, honest, angry, suffering Job, who has been proud and impatient in his arguments, kneels before the living God.

> I had heard of you . . . but now my eye sees you,
> Therefore, I despise myself . . . and repent in dust and ashes.

And that is the true ending. That is the original ending, still leaving us with a paradox, a dilemma to cope with. But because we are humans, someone, at some later time, gave the story a happy ending. The horrible comforters are roundly condemned. And God restores all the fortunes of Job.

What can these forty-two chapters, written about two and a half thousand years ago, mean for us today? There are perhaps three things that we can pick up.

1. Faithful Doubt

We often talk as though doubt were the opposite of faith. But that is not so. They are on the same side. That is why it is right to question our faith. When doubts come to mind, sometimes very easily, that is part of growing up in the faith. Do not stifle them. It is good to ask questions. 'I wonder if this bit of the Bible is historically accurate?' 'Is that particular interpretation, which I learned in Sunday School, believable now?' These are questions of faith and help us to grow as Christians.

The opposite of faith has to be superstition – that which believes in everything and anything, uncritically, unquestioningly – the lottery, astrology, throwing a pinch of salt over your shoulder, and a whole lot of quasi-religious acts, too.

But doubting and unbelief and questions and even anger against God are all part of the life of faith. We need not be frightened to argue with God. It was the soppy unquestioning comforters who in the end were condemned. And Job was the one who struggled through oceans of doubt and was met by the living God.

Do not be ashamed of doubt or questions or anger. They are part of the life of faith.

2. Suffering and God

After all the forty-two chapters we have no easy answers, no soft solutions, no smart answers, no short cuts and no cheap miracles. Suffering is a hard fact.

The book of Job reminds us that there is much suffering in the world. Our pain may be severe, but other people are also suffering.

- grief for a life's partner,
- the emptiness of utter depression,
- unyielding physical pain,
- debilitating and wasting disease,
- a once-hopeful relationship torn apart,
- fear, violence, poverty, injustice . . .

All these and more are part of the suffering of the world. Job stands on one side of incarnation, crucifixion, resurrection, and the pouring out of the Spirit, and we are on the other. We know, as Job did not, that God in Jesus Christ understands human suffering from the inside and carries it in his heart still. The old Scottish paraphrase, number 58, a paraphrase of Hebrews 4:14–end, says:

> Our fellow-sufferer yet retains
> A fellow-feeling of our pains;
> And still remembers in the skies
> His tears, his agonies, and cries.[3]

God suffers with us.

3. The Powerlessness of God

God does not live in a minstrels' gallery, nor in any remote or inaccessible place. Nor does God play games with us – that was dramatic and poetic licence.

God is one who draws near to men and women. We so often think in naive Sunday School ways. We still sometimes think of a God who is on tap for us to use or not, as some magician in the sky who will hand out punishments or rewards in a fairly capricious way. But that is pagan. That is superstition. That is unchristian.

God is the one who created this universe out of love. God has filled this world with life and love and laughter, and asks us to enjoy the gifts of his love in freedom.

But in giving us freedom as part of the gift of creation, *God surrenders power.* For God will not act against our freedom, our freedom to make war and injustice, to hate and destroy.

For generations, for centuries, we have not understood. And so God himself came in Jesus to call us into free and loving relationship with him. Jesus has entered into that frailty and suffering. In our most anguished questioning, we cry with him and he with us, 'My God, why have you forsaken me?'

The book of Job is poetic theology. It is truth from powerful fable. But our faith comes from historical reality.

- God in Christ suffers and dies with us and for us.
- God in Christ endured the outrage of human dying and death itself.
- God in Christ embraces us with his deathless love and his unending kindness.
- God invites us to live with him and to love with him and to take risks with him.

I do not know what you have to face.

I do not know

- what burdens you carry
- what problems you live with
- what suffering you have to shoulder
- what burdens you bear
- what temptations you may face

- what decisions you must take
- what joys you may be given
- what tears you may shed

but I believe that whatever you may have to face, God in Christ walks that path and holds you by the hand.

NOTES

1. This sermon was first preached in Rondebosch Presbyterian Church, Cape Town, South Africa.
2. The title of a novel by Muriel Spark.
3. *Church Hymnary* (third edition) 295, Scottish Paraphrases, 58.

6

Losing Faith

A SERMON ON DOUBT

Readings:	*1 Samuel 17:31–49*
	Mark 4:35–41
Season:	*Second Sunday after Pentecost*

'Art thou afraid his power shall fail when comes thy evil day?'[1] These words are from a well-known Scottish paraphrase. Are you frightened that if something awful happens, God won't be strong enough to deal with it?

Here are two very well-known stories. There is something about them that makes me think of big armchairs, and storybooks, and a soothing adult voice reading to me. We enjoy the old familiar stories. For we know that whatever the excitement, all will end wonderfully well. The giant will be slain. Wee David will triumph. The storm will be calmed and no-one will be seasick, let alone drowned.

But they are, in fact, very scary stories. And they are only bearable *because* we know that everything does come right. The Goliath story has on the one side someone of immense height and strength and experience. He is protected by the heaviest metal armour and armed with mighty weapons. David is young and fit, but he is wearing ordinary clothes. He cannot bear the weight of the armour and is therefore unprotected. His only weapon is the same sling he uses when caring for the family sheep, a sort of catapult. The whole story is rigged against him. And yet little David, with God, is more than a match for the arrogant might of Goliath and his cumbersome armour.

The storm on the Sea of Galilee is another frightening story made comfortable by its familiarity and the knowledge that all will be well. But again, to live through the event would have been terrifying, with the sleeping carpenter adding both alarm and insult to the seasoned fishermen. How could *he* sleep through it, when the professionals could not? How could he abandon them? How could he? But with Jesus all is well. And so both stories end and we can stretch in the comfort of our armchairs and go and put on the kettle before we return to the real world.

Last week, I was at a meeting of office-bearers in this congregation, the leaders of the Sunday Club. We met to do business but we met also to eat cakes and drink coffee and enjoy each other's company and fellowship. We talked business and gossip and told jokes and swapped holiday hopes and then, quite naturally, we moved into faith and theology.

- How do I know that my faith will be strong enough?
- Will God protect me from evil?
- I can only operate if I feel God is looking down from heaven to look after *me*.
- If anything happened to me, or, worse, to my children, I'd lose my faith.
- What about dreadful massacres of children, such as happened in Dunblane?
- I'm frightened of losing my faith.
- I'm frightened of losing God.

We all joined in. And all of us felt vulnerable, especially for our children, but also for ourselves. How far does suffering have to go before we break? All of us were fearful of meeting a breaking point which would leave us without faith, without God, and alone.

Most of us have such Fears

Someone was joking with me the other day about being a chocoholic. She told me that nine people out of ten love chocolate and the tenth person is a liar. Anyone who is not frightened of extreme pain or disaster or the death of a loved one is either lacking in imagination or is a liar. We are all frightened.

Remember Jesus in the garden, sweating so that the drops were running off him like drops of blood. Remember him saying, 'God, let this not happen. Please don't let it happen.' Remember him on the cross shouting, 'God, *God*, why have you abandoned me?' And he died, apparently still believing, but not knowing, that it would end well.

Oh yes. We are all frightened. All of us. So share your fears. Christians are not supposed to be without fear. We are human. And it may be by sharing our fear rather than our faith that we may help others to know Jesus. It may be by sharing our weakness rather than our strength that we point to the strength of the Lord. It may be by sharing our vulnerability, rather than our competence, that we can encourage others to believe that God is a God for small people and sinful people and broken people.

Faith is not about being Certain

Faith is about hanging in there against the odds. Certainty would be, well, certain. In certainty, there would be no room for faith.

Faith is about not knowing, not seeing, not being sure, but still saying, I trust.

My favourite story about this is from the book of Daniel. Whether the story actually happened as history, or is only a story, does not matter. It is in truth a great story of faith.

Daniel's friends, Shadrach, Meshach and Abednego, who were true to the teachings of their faith and refused to bow down to the great Babylonian idol, were about to be thrust into the burning fiery furnace. One of the great classic statements of faith was made, 'If our God whom we serve is able to deliver us from the furnace of blazing fire, and out of your hand, O king, let him deliver us. *But if not*, be it known to you, O king, that we will not serve your gods and we will not worship the golden statue that you have set up.'[2]

The story tells of the furnace being so hot that the guards who tended it were slain by the heat. But when Daniel's friends were thrust in, they were miraculously saved. But *before* the horror, before the pain and fear, before the imminence of death, the great statement of faith was made: 'If our God whom we serve is able to deliver us from the furnace of blazing fire, and out of your hand, O king, let him deliver us. *But if not*.' But if not . . . there is faith for you. Clinging on by your fingernails in the face of insolent might.

Faith Increases Sensitivity to Others

Faith makes us *more* aware, not less, of other people. That is why it is right that we should tremble at the massacre in the primary school at Dunblane – for other people's children. That is why we shiver with fear and weep for the fifteen young backpackers who were burned to death by an arsonist in Childers in Queensland.

That is why we question the randomness of cancer. That is why we find it hard to accept the scourge of cystic fibrosis. Faith increases sensitivity to all suffering. That is why any congregation worth its salt will have Traidcraft or Tear Fund stalls. They will support missionary schools, colleges and hospitals. Faith linked to fear produces sensitivity and sympathy and action.

Are you afraid his power shall fail when your evil day comes? Are you frightened that if something awful happens, God won't be strong enough to deal with it? When we were discussing this the other night, people wanted to know what I felt. It was important to know what the minister believed.

I hope people are not too shocked to know that I also fear the pain or the hurt that may kill my faith. I also find it hard to understand the apparent randomness of cancer or cystic fibrosis. I find natural disasters, flood, famine, volcano and earthquake difficult to accept. But when I was pressed by these young Sunday School teachers to answer their questions honestly, I felt I had to try. In a nutshell, the questions and answers went like this:

'Is God there?' Yes, but less powerfully, in our sense of the word, than we want and more full of suffering love and strong support than we could imagine.

'Are we protected from disaster?' Probably not. There is no spell or prayer or mantra that offers any sort of magical protection.

'Will God be there for us?' Yes, but not necessarily the way we want.

'Can any good come out of suffering?' Yes. Yes. Yes. Ida Scudder was only a teenager from high school when she came from the USA to keep house for her father in Ranipet, southern India. He was a missionary doctor, but because of Hindu and Muslim rules and customs, he was not allowed to act as an obstetrician. On one fateful evening, the young Ida was asked to come to help at three difficult deliveries. She was young. She was shy. She had no medical training. She refused to go. In the morning she sent word asking after the young mothers, only to learn that all three of them had died in childbirth during the night. Shocked and distraught, she vowed to return to the USA and train as a doctor. From that terrible night there was built the Christian Medical College and Hospital. It is the glory of Vellore and has saved countless lives – in some ways because of the tragic deaths of three young women in childbirth a hundred years ago. From the tragedy of their suffering, Dr Ida Scudder built a haven of healing, care and compassion, and of medical excellence unsurpassed in India.

And to this I cling with all the faith that I have. What God did with the cross of his own dear son, he can do with the crosses of all his children.

NOTES

1. *Church Hymnary* (third edition) 394, Scottish Paraphrases, 22.
2. Daniel 3:16.

Touching the World –
through Politics

7

Destiny and Dedication

THE SCOTTISH REFERENDUM, 1997

<table>
<tr><td>Readings:</td><td>Exodus 2:1–10
1 Peter 2:9–10
Luke 2:25–35</td></tr>
<tr><td>Occasion:</td><td>This sermon was preached in September 1997
on the Sunday which followed the death of
Diana, Princess of Wales, the Sunday which
preceded the Scottish National Referendum.</td></tr>
</table>

'You are a chosen race, a royal priesthood, a holy nation' (1 Peter 2:9).

Over this last puzzling and harrowing week, we have heard much about destiny. What is destiny? In November 1948 a child was born. An official announcement went something like this:

This morning Her Royal Highness the Princess Elizabeth was safely delivered of a son. Her Royal Highness and the infant prince are both well.

His name was Charles Philip Arthur George, the Prince of Wales – a man born to be King. That was his destiny. And when Diana Spencer married him, people who watched the service on television thought that she would be Queen. But it was not to be.

Let us be clear from the start that destiny is nothing to do with a dumb and unfeeling God moving people about on a gigantic chessboard, conceding a castle and a bishop to gain a Queen. No. Destiny is more to do with what a person has the potential to do if all the circumstances are right – circumstances that may include family, upbringing, education, health, opportunity, external factors and also the package of genes with which one is born.

Whatever cocktail of circumstances there were, and we may never know the whole truth, the man born to be King and Diana Spencer were to be united in a marriage which, with hindsight, had tragedy built into it from the start. But let us not blame *God* for human tragedy, a tragedy which was of *their* making, but a tragedy in which *we all* shared, with our demand for glittering icons and our relentless intrusive desire to know more.

So for all the talk of destiny, Diana will not be Queen and it remains to be seen if Charles will be King.

You see, destiny is not chance. Destiny may be all the potential we are born with and born into, but *essentially* destiny is to do with choice.

When Moses was born, he was destined to die. All baby boys were being killed as they were born. It was impossible that he could survive. When I was in the National Museum of Cairo, I saw a number of very ancient baskets with hoods and lids. In delight, I thought I had discovered the prototype cradle, only to be told that these were child coffins. Dead babies were placed in them and they floated down the Nile. And suddenly I was powerfully aware of the Moses story. It wasn't any old basket his mother had chosen, it was a coffin she would put him in, but she would put in a live baby and trust him to God.

We are told that his mother kept the birth a secret and fed him and cuddled him and then hid him in the famous Moses' basket. But it was a standard coffin. The Egyptian princess should have reported the slave child and had him killed. But she chose not to

– was it the cry of hunger that moved her? Or a sudden smile on the baby's face? What made her heart turn over and decide to keep him? And clever sister Miriam negotiating that the child's own mother should be his wet nurse . . . And so the scene is set for Moses to be an Egyptian prince instead of a dead slave. It is a long and fascinating story, and, in the end, Moses is the one to lead the Hebrew people out of slavery into the wilderness, there to forge them into a nation, so that when they entered the promised land, they were not the demoralised rabble that had left, always complaining and bitter about everything, but a reborn people, organised and disciplined, willing to take responsibility for themselves. The baby born to die had a different destiny. Indeed, those of us in the Jewish/Christian/Muslim tradition would say that Moses, apparently intended for death, had *truly* fulfilled God's intention for him.

This week is a week of destiny for this nation, our nation, for the people of Scotland. Events last week have largely over-shadowed what is arguably the most significant moment in the history of Scotland for nearly three hundred years. It is now time that whatever grief or guilt or anger we may be nursing over the death of Diana, Princess of Wales, we must not be deflected by the blanket media coverage of something for which we are *not* responsible from that for which we so obviously *are* responsible. We must seize now our choice and our destiny.

Most people here who went to school in Scotland have some dates burned into infant memories. For example, there was in the year 1503 the marriage of the Thistle and the Rose, which brought about a century later in 1603 the Union of the Crowns, when James VI of Scotland succeeded Queen Elizabeth of England. Another century later in 1707 the Union of Parliaments took place. Much that was distinctive in Scottish life began to decline as our culture was subsumed into the more powerful language and culture of the south. Of course we embraced some changes and assented to others, and we should blame no-one but ourselves.

A distinctive voice of less than five million among about fifty-five million is difficult to maintain. Perhaps the greatest contribution the Scots gave to the world, as did the Irish, was in the waves of immigrants to other lands – most leaving not by choice but by necessity. And there is the old joke that Scotland provides the heads of departments in Whitehall; I don't know whether that is still true, but what is true is that in the present government it is Scotland who educated the Prime Minister, the Chancellor of the Exchequer, the Foreign Secretary and others.

This week, we are being allowed to choose whether or not we are willing to take responsibility for some of our affairs, for our own destiny. This is not independence. It is not breaking up the union. It is being willing to take responsibility for many areas of life, including education and health, and being accountable for them. Some of you may want that and others of you will not. It is a personal decision and a private vote. But we must be clear about this. If you intend to vote 'yes', then be willing to make it work with support and money and commitment. If you intend to vote 'no', then do not ever again complain that you had no choice or blame unnamed people far away in Whitehall.

When God chose to save the Hebrew people from slavery, he chose a baby. Moses, in childhood and adulthood, was guided through stormy and terrible times.

When God chose to save the world, another baby was born – not a prince, not even born to be a prince, but an ordinary baby born to working-class folks. He was very ordinary, born to be a joiner. Only the old man Simeon, so near to his own death, saw something that was special:

For my eyes have seen your salvation which you have prepared . . .
a light . . . a glory . . .
   This child is destined to be a sign that will be opposed . . .
and a sword will pierce your own soul too.[1]

And the child, sent to love the world and save the world, was
executed because the people he came to save could not, would
not, accept the changes that were demanded.

Before we rush to condemn the people of the time, remember
how dangerously radical were the words of Jesus. Remember how
disturbing and painful were the changes he called us to make.
Recall how he criticised the establishment. Think of how he upset
the moral conventions and how he made impossible demands. He
was a hard person to follow if you were to take him seriously;
perhaps that is why he gathered the poorer sections of society and
the outcasts around him – they had little to lose and much to gain.

Incredibly and wonderfully, he promised them, and us, a place
in his Kingdom. Not by wealth nor by achievement, not by
advancement nor by effort, do we win a place in the Kingdom.
But by love, God's love, are we given a place in the Kingdom,
there to learn slowly, joyfully and painfully the secret life of God's
Kingdom.

It is wonderful to feel the love of God accepting us and forgiving
us and loving us. It is inexpressibly good to feel those arms of
love around us, whispering words of such gentle comfort that we
want to relax there and weep like tired children in their mother's
arms.

But God's Kingdom is not just about comfort. It is also about
change and choice and destiny. Within the powerful and em-
powering love of God we learn that we are engaged to live lives
of truth and mercy, service and faith, re-evaluating much of what
the world counts as good and sitting loose to the conventions of

this age. It is our responsibility to try to build in this nation a more Christian society, with concern for others written into the fabric of our lives.

This week, let us not be obsessed by the destiny of a dead princess or a living, but undoubtedly troubled, prince. Let us not live vicariously in someone else's life or tragedy. It is *our destiny* for which we have responsibility:

> You are a chosen race, a royal priesthood, a holy nation, God's own people, in order that you may proclaim the mighty acts of him who called you out of darkness into his marvellous light.[2]

NOTES

1. Luke 2:30, 34, 35.
2. 1 Peter 2:9.

8

A Rustle of Dry Leaves

THE SCOTTISH GENERAL ELECTION, 1999

Readings:	*Acts 7:54 – 8:1*
	1 Peter 2:2–10
	John 14:1–14
Season:	*Fifth Sunday of Easter*
Occasion:	*This sermon was preached on 2 May 1999, the Sunday before the election of the Scottish Parliament.*

If I walk to church, which I enjoy doing if the weather is kind, I pass a house round the corner from us which has a lovely beech hedge. In the summer it is beautiful with bright green soft leaves fluttering in the wind. In the autumn it is gorgeous with yellow, gold and copper colours. It is one of the few deciduous plants which holds on to its dying leaves, and as I walk home in the winter, in the dark, I hear the comforting whisper of the leaves as they rustle in the wind. But my favourite time of year is now, in the spring. For the brave old leaves are still there, hard and dry, but the brilliant new young leaves of radiant yellow-green shine through the old winter foliage of rust and copper. First there is a small area of green with new leaves gently unfurling, then there is a patchwork effect, with equal areas of rusty old leaves and the fresh tender new leaves. And then as the new and young and

47

vigorous inevitably take over, the old leaves of last year finally bow out and flutter to the ground. The comfort of the past gives way to the pull of the future.

The pull of the future is the connection between the three readings we have had today. I'd like to look at the three readings briefly, then work out what this may mean for us today.

In the book of Acts, we read of the stoning of Stephen, the first Christian martyr.

- It was a turning point for the church, making it see that following Jesus was not a cushy number, but a hard and lonely reality.

- It was a turning point for Saul, implacably opposed to the Christian movement, but influenced in spite of himself by Stephen's death.

- It was the end of an easy Jewish Christianity and the start of persecution, of the scattering of the disciples, and *therefore* the start of a wider church and the beginning of a wider mission movement.

Truly the blood of the martyrs is the seed of the church. The past, with all its tragedy, gives a doorway to the future, with all its terror and its opportunity. The pull of the future is stronger than the comfort of the past.

The letter of Peter tells of the rejected stone becoming the chief cornerstone. The young Christians are reminded of their role as the new Israel. They are to regard their suffering as evidence not of rejection, but of a call to new responsibility. Following Jesus will lead to new life. The people who were nonentities are now part of a royal priesthood, a dedicated nation, God's own people. The past is behind them. They must give way to the pull of the future.

That famous chapter of John's gospel is often read at funeral services, so powerful is its message concerning the future. Jesus is trying to explain that his departure will open up a new relationship between him and his disciples. His earthly mission, after his imminent death, will be accomplished through them.

They are slow to understand – as we are now and would have been then. They are unwilling to face the inevitable, always hoping and believing that rabbits will be pulled out of hats, and chestnuts from the fire. But Jesus is uncompromising.

- I am going to my Father . . .
- You know the way . . .
- I am the way, the truth and the life. . .
- The person who has faith in me will do what I do . . . and will do greater things still, because I am going to the Father.

In other words, Jesus was saying to his friends and disciples that his mission here on earth would be accomplished, would be finished, not by him, but by us.

The disciples did not want change. They did not want to be disturbed. They did not want to understand. But they could not halt time. They could not live in the past. They had to bow to the inevitable pull of the future, with its insecurities and uncertainties.

We often read the scriptures as if everyone knew what they were doing at all times. We often want to believe that people understood exactly where they fitted into God's plan of salvation – super heroes, everyone! I cannot believe that that is true. Much of the time God works with very ordinary human beings who dither and doubt, who swither and backtrack, who are sometimes believing but often haven't the faintest idea that God is working in them and through them and with them.

The disciples and Saul, who later became Paul, were exactly like that. But God relentlessly pulled them into the future.

Life with Christ is not just picnics in Galilee; it is letting Jesus go, and taking responsibility. Life in the early church was not just praying behind locked doors, it was acknowledging that Christ is Lord before a hostile judiciary. In *our* church life, we are summoned to put the past behind and step forward to the future. In the Church of Scotland we can be dominated by the past. And the older I get, and the longer my memory is, the more I become like that, too! It is interesting to know what happened in the past, but Christ calls us to the future. Are we prepared for the church of the future? Are we willing to change, to adapt, to die?

This week as a nation, we stand at a new future. On Thursday we elect the first Scottish Parliament for nearly three hundred years. It is an exciting time. In September 1997, I remember standing here and preaching about devolution and destiny. And I want to say again what I said then:

> Destiny is not chance. Destiny is all that potential we are born with and born into, but *essentially* destiny is to do with choice.

We can now take responsibility for many aspects of the life of our nation. And we can choose people who will make it work and who will be accountable to us.

I do not care how you vote. But I beg you to go out on Thursday and vote. I have just come back from Australia, where it is compulsory to vote. Perhaps the privilege and responsibility of voting are taken so seriously because many people arrived in that country through injustice or hardship or poverty or persecution. I know a lot of people in Edinburgh who can't be bothered to vote.

- If ever you have complained about 'them'.
- If you have ever moaned about nameless people 'out there'.

- If you have ever agitated about bad roads, impossible parking, poor schooling, worsening health care, long waiting lists, pollution in the cities, high taxation.

If you have, then you have a duty to vote.

Jesus forced the disciples to face the future. Saul was pulled into the future by the death of Stephen. Today, we must look to the future with faith and determination. God will not abandon the church nor the people of Scotland. The question is whether you are willing to put the past behind you, and move forward in church and nation? It is from the future that the risen Christ beckons.

9

Saltires and Celebration

THE OPENING OF THE SCOTTISH PARLIAMENT, 1999

Readings:	*Isaiah 49:1–13*
	1 Peter 2:9–10
	John 1:35–42
Occasion:	*This sermon was preached on 4 July 1999, the Sunday following the opening of the new Scottish Parliament.*

As I mentioned a few weeks ago, I am the proud possessor of a new computer. It is far more powerful than I can understand and it has more memory than all of us here put together. I secretly suspect it is more intelligent than I am, but I don't like to talk about that. One area of it, which I have not yet learned to use, is the e-mail. So imagine my surprise on Friday morning, when I went into the study to write this sermon, and I found the screen alive with shooting stars and multicoloured rainbows and fish swimming across the screen, and, yes, blue and white saltires flying all over the place. As I watched in amazement, a message began to come up on the screen. This is how it was headed:

To:
saintsalive@stmichaels.co.edinburgh.scotland
From:
andrew@patronsaints.cloudnine.seventhheaven.co.eternity

Now the assumption is that Andrew, patron saint of Scotland, never wrote a letter. Perhaps he did not know how to write. But here, unmistakably, was a letter from Andrew, our patron saint, sent to us from heaven. Somehow, it had come to earth via my magic new machine. This is how it went on.

Grace to you, love and peace from Andrew, apostle and friend of the Lord. I rejoice with all my brothers and sisters in Scotland on this special occasion. I join with them in prayers for their wonderful new Parliament, and call upon them to exercise their citizenship in earth and heaven as good Christians.

It is many years in your human time since the Lord, my friend and saviour, called me from following the family business of fishing. I was glad to follow Jesus because I knew, although I could not explain then, that he was unique. There was no-one like him in the world. We were all in love with him – more than that, we were alight with his love and his faith in us.

Perhaps I should start by confessing that I found it very hard to be in the shadow of my big brother Simon. I did love him but he was always so pigheaded and stubborn and attention-seeking. I found it hard to be a good disciple. I would want to ask Jesus about something really important, and just as I had worked out how to ask it, Simon would jump in with both feet and ask *his* question first. So my annoying big brother gets mentioned a lot in the gospel stories that you have, and I get scarcely a mention.

But I want you to know that I am so pleased that the Lord has thought me worthy to look after three great countries. There is Greece, such a cradle of education and philosophy and literature. Then there is Russia, that great country, that great Christian country, returning gradually to its true vocation as a land dedicated to Christ and his Kingdom. I have had to work hard on Russia. And there is Scotland, tiny little Scotland. When I was assigned to Scotland I was so pleased. For one thing it is a manageable size. I prefer small countries. And for another there was so much water it immediately made me feel at home – I am still a fisherman at heart. But most of all, I loved the Scots because although they often find it hard to show or express their emotions (a bit as I was on earth), when they fell in love with Christ and his Kingdom, it was total. There were no half-measures.

I have confessed to you my jealousy (when I was on earth) of my brother Simon Peter. I was even exasperated to find that he had insisted on being crucified upside down. How like him! So brave, so faithful – and so bumptious! I did not really care how I went to the Lord as long as I went quickly – to see his dear face, to meet his eyes and to hear him say, 'Well done, Andrew.' As it turned out, they crucified me in the form of the letter X, the first letter of Christ's name in Greek.

The reason I tell you all this is that on Thursday, 1 July 1999, in your time, I had the last laugh. Even my brother Simon Peter laughed with me in heaven and acknowledged that after all these years I had finally outdone him. For in Scotland on that day, there were more of *my* crosses flying than anything I had ever dreamt of, and even my dear exasperating big brother had to admit that this was one occasion when I had the last laugh!

But I did not write to tell you that. I am writing because I, as your patron saint, have a message for you all. In fact I have three messages.

First, it is truly wonderful that you celebrated your new Parliament so well. The words 'There shall be a Scottish Parliament' thrilled me as much as if in my time on earth we had been able to have our own Parliament instead of the hated Roman law. People said that it was a just law. Maybe it was, but it was not our own Jewish law and therefore we could not rejoice in it. We had the dream of our own Parliament, and then the hope. Some of us had the belief, but never in my time was there a promise, let alone the reality. So I, Andrew, your patron saint, rejoice that you have your Parliament.

But, I solemnly charge you, with liberty goes commitment. With freedom goes duty. With privilege goes responsibility. As Christian people of Scotland, it is your joyful task to make sure that Christian values are at the heart of the political process. You must put Christian ethics at the centre of discussion. You must ensure that Christian generosity is central in planning for schools and health care, and the welfare of the elderly and the vulnerable. This is something that only you can do. Do not complain that decisions are not with you. For now they are. If you want 'wisdom and justice, compassion and integrity' to flourish, you must work and pray for it. And it is your Christian faith and your Christian commitment that will shape your nation – or not. Christian freedom requires Christian commitment.

The second message I want to share with you concerns nationhood and diversity. An island people are sometimes too pure, too insular. They may be racially homogenous. They may have one language and one culture. But this nation has three ancient mother tongues, Gaelic, Scots and English, as well as many new ones. It has a diversity of culture and a richness of music, art and literature. It is innovative and enquiring. It is rich in agriculture and fishery. It is democratic in education, the law and health care. It has entrepreneurial skills and has been celebrated for business, banking and industry.

And now it has many more new Scots; they come from the Indian subcontinent and from the Caribbean, from Italy and Greece, from many African countries and from England. Even this week more have arrived from Kosovo. They are not strangers or aliens. They are new Scots. They come to this northern land as some folk brought my bones so long ago, to find refuge and peace. So, for my sake, welcome these new Scots. They are part of your family. Get to know them. Share with them. Learn from them. They have much to give. They are part of God's loving purpose for your nation and part of your nation.

Third, and last, I share with you a puzzle and concern that I have. It is about the future of Christianity in Scotland. I still cannot find out what my dear Lord Jesus expects or wants us to do. Even in heaven all is not clear, you know! I had assumed, we all had assumed, that the glorious Christian message of Christ's redeeming love and saving grace would sweep through the whole world with love and power. And it did.

But there are still the ancient religions and more modern faiths. Other 'isms' abound – materialism, secularism, agnosticism and apathy. Even in the Christian church there is a fair measure of those, especially apathy. Once upon a time there were many who worshipped on the Lord's day and celebrated his glorious resurrection. Now fewer and fewer worship and I wonder what the Lord has planned for Scotland. So I, Andrew, confess that I am puzzled.

All I can say to you, my dear people, is that I have often been puzzled in the presence of the Lord, puzzled but trusting. Once Jesus asked me and my friend Philip to feed a large crowd – the two of us! There were at least five thousand there and me with not even enough money to feed the lot of us. So I looked around and there was a wee laddie with some scraps of bread and salted fish. He was offering some to a friend and when he caught my eye he grinned and held out a crust for me. So I took him by the hand and brought him to Jesus. Well, the rest is history . . . You'll have read about it.

So I don't know whether Scotland will become a Christian nation again or not. Just as I didn't know whether those people would be fed or not. It's never been my way to ask too many questions. I just do as Jesus asks. And things do come right.

So live as Christians and love as Christians. Share your faith when you can. And when you can't, pray for your neighbours. Have faith. Be true to the Lord Jesus. You are a holy people. Scotland is in the hands of our blessed saviour. I pray for you constantly. I, Andrew, pray for you, for your kirk and your people and for your new Parliament.

And so, I say farewell. The grace of the Lord Jesus Christ be with you all.

10

Crying in the Wilderness

HUMAN RIGHTS[1]

Readings:	Isaiah 61:1–4, 8–11
	1 Thessalonians 5:16–24
	John 1:6–8, 19–28
Season:	Third Sunday in Advent

John the Baptist said, 'I am the voice of one crying out in the wilderness' (John 1:23).

1. Here is a picture: John the Baptist

He was a thin wiry man, gaunt, sinewy, and tough as old boots. He wore rough clothes. He ate from the desert – wild honey and locust beans. An uncompromising person, but with bags of charisma, a holy man, and when the time was right people came out of the towns to hear him preach and teach. They listened to him scolding them and they took it. Hearts were turned and many went down to the banks of the Jordan river to have the waters poured over them as a sign that they would live a new and different life. Some would look and listen and watch – perhaps moved but not quite ready to make that final step. But they loved to watch and listen. The crowds flocked to hear him.

Eventually a deputation was sent from the *high heid yins*[2] of Jerusalem. The priests and Levites were sent to make an official investigation. After all, religion was all right, but this preacher was stirring up the people. If his preaching concerned their souls, that would be in order. If, however, it upset the delicate balance between the Jewish hierarchy and the Roman occupying forces then it had to be dealt with – and the sooner the better. So the *high heid yins* went out to see John with their list of questions.

- Question: are you the Messiah?
  Answer: I'm not the Messiah.

- Question: are you Elijah?
  Answer: no.

- Question: are you the prophet we've been waiting for?
  Answer: no.

- Question: who are you then?
  Answer: *I am the voice of one crying out in the wilderness.*

What good is a voice crying out in the *wilderness*? There is no-one to hear. There will be no effect. What difference does one voice make?

2. *Here is another picture: Rosa Parks*

In the 1950s a black woman got on the bus in Little Rock, Arkansas. She was tired and she sat down gratefully at the back of the vehicle, the area set aside for blacks. But more people got on and, as required by the then laws of the state, she was obliged to give up her seat for a white person who got on. And for the first time in the history of the state a black person said 'no'. She refused to give up her seat. There were riots and huge political unrest and the new freedom fight began, the fight that caused death and martyrs and brought Martin Luther King to head up the long battle for civil rights and liberties for all people.

But it started because of one woman, Rosa Parks. *I am the voice of one crying out in the wilderness.*

3. Here is another picture: an unknown Indonesian

In the 1980s a man in Indonesia was put in prison along with many others. Possibly he had been working for the freedom of East Timor. Maybe he was a Roman Catholic priest. Maybe he was a Baptist pastor. I just do not know what he was nor what he had done that put him in prison. But I do know that he was on a list of people who were adopted by Amnesty International in the Christmas of 1991. He had done nothing that was criminal of any sort but had protested peacefully. And you and I in St Michael's were asked to send him, along with several other prisoners of conscience, cards with a message of encouragement. That was the year I carefully stuck my address labels on the back of each envelope after I had signed the card.

Three months later, *I* received a card. A wedding card. Was that because he could not speak English? Or was that a ploy to get a message out of prison to me? I couldn't read it. It was in another language. But then I realised that there were numbers in his letter to me. He had written in a kind of code, using Bible references as a way of conveying his message.

- Philippians 4:14
- Philippians 1:3, 4
- Matthew 25:36
- Psalm 126:4, 5
- Galatians 6:9

Once I had put in the appropriate texts, his message to me read like this:

Rev. Margaret,

Greetings in the name of Jesus. It was kind of you to share my distress.

I thank my God every time I remember you, constantly praying with joy in every one of my prayers for all of you.

I was naked and you gave me clothing. I was sick and you took care of me. I was in prison and you visited me.

Restore our fortunes, O Lord, like the water courses in the Negeb. May those who sow in tears reap with shouts of joy.

So let us not grow weary in doing what is right, for we will reap at harvest time, if we do not give up.

Immanuel – God is with us.

When you and I sign cards, as we shall be doing in a very short time, we are tempted to think, 'What's the use?' This is the use: *I am the voice of one crying out in the wilderness.*

4. Here is another picture: a twelve-year-old from Pakistan

In 1995 in Pakistan a Christian boy was accused of a crime he did not commit and was sentenced to death. Amnesty International took up his case and many people signed a petition asking for his release. The petition was available in this congregation and some people did sign it. Others did not. The reasons were mixed.

- I don't know enough about it.
- I don't like meddling in another country's affairs.
- One signature will not make all the difference.

I am the voice of one crying out in the wilderness. But there were, mercifully many voices crying and the boy was set free.

5. *Here is another picture: a darkened room*

Here is an anonymous man, woman, child, in a prison cell. No wrong has been done. No crime has been committed. But the person spoke out against insolent might. Words were spoken for justice, for freedom, for democracy, for the right to worship, for the right to be educated, for the right to vote. And now that person is in prison, isolated, without proper clothing, in the dark, deprived of books and proper food and clean water, perhaps tortured and raped, certainly without visitors or legal help. Who will help? Can anyone in the world? *I am the voice of one crying out in the wilderness.*

6. *Here is one last picture: an Edinburgh congregation*

This congregation, today, will be asked to sign some cards to send to political prisoners like that. We know their names. We know that they have been selected by Amnesty International. We know that they have done no violence nor have they committed any crime. And here are some of the things going through your minds.

- But it's late and I'll miss my lunch.
- I'll miss the bus.
- I have the grandchildren coming today.
- I'm going out this afternoon.
- What is one signature worth?

I am the voice of one crying out in the wilderness.

The society to which God calls us this Christmas is not one of glittering palaces and opulent wealth. Nor is it of lavish spending and selfish indulgence. It is of justice, truth, kindness and generosity. It will be marked by freedom to captives, good news to the oppressed, and the jubilee of debts cancelled. A far cry from the Christmas rush. Today *hear* the voice. Today *be* the voice. *The voice of one crying out in the wilderness.*

NOTES

1. Annually in St Michael's on a Sunday near to Human Rights Day, members of the congregation send cards to prisoners of conscience selected by Amnesty International.
2. Literally, 'high head ones' meaning those who have authority and power.

Keeping in Touch –
with the Church

11

Can These Stones Live?

RESTORING A BUILDING

Readings:	*2 Chronicles 6:12–21*
	1 Peter 2:4–10
	Matthew 12:1–8
Occasion:	*This sermon was preached on 23 January 1999*
	after ten years of fundraising and work to
	restore and paint the inside of the church
	building and halls.

On this very special day in the history of St Michael's, all of us are delighting in the warmth, the sparkle, the fresh paint and the new carpet. We delight in the beauty of the sanctuary and our praise has shown it.

The Old Testament reading concerns a similar gorgeous situation. All Israel was gathered for the opening of the Temple. David had planned it. Solomon had built it. Devastating taxation had raised the money. Forced labour had built it. Forests were cut down. Metals and precious stones were mined. Craftsmen had laboured. Yet higher taxation had been laid on the people. And finally, the Temple was ready. And it is spine-tingling stuff. All Israel was there. The podium was for Solomon the King, and on it he prostrates himself before the living God and says:

> But will God indeed reside with mortals on earth? Even heaven and the highest heaven cannot contain you, how much less this house that I have built . . . Hear the plea . . . of your people Israel, when they pray towards this place . . . Hear and forgive.

Most people here love this building with deep passion and with steady commitment. Some are so caught up with love of the building that it is difficult to disentangle what the church is from what the building is.

Some people here have never known what another church is, except on holiday. For they have been born into this congregation, baptised in this font, nurtured within the congregation, growing to maturity here. Everything they know about church, they have learned here. Some here had parents or grandparents who worshipped in the old Iron Church and who have stories about the funeral of the first minister, Dr Wilson. Some here attended the marriage of the second minister, John Hamilton. Several have stories of how their parents and other relatives worked to pay off the original debt in the 1890s.

And some of us love it, not just in its magnificent entirety, but inch by painful inch. For we have scrubbed tiles, sanded walls, patched plaster, painted cornices, scaled scaffolding, made curtains, re-laid paving slabs outside, swept leaves, mown the grass, and, with frozen fingers, painted outside railings.

And some have raised money by holding car boot sales, organising coffee mornings, running the marvellous local charity shops. And some have dug deep into savings, giving up a holiday, a new coat, a new car, to give to the church.

> Thy saints take pleasure in her stones,
> Her very dust to them is dear.[1]

It is not a sin to love the building in which we worship. We praise and thank God for it. Most of us have had a blessing from

God within this place. Children have played with confidence as though they own the place. Adults have walked reverently, knowing that they do *not* own this place. We have rejoiced to know that we stand within God's loving purpose and unending kindness. We praise and thank God for it.

When Jesus walked with his disciples through the corn fields, they broke the law. No. That gives entirely the wrong impression. They did not break the law as one picks up a parking fine. They engaged in a positive act of civil disobedience – civil and religious disobedience. It was done deliberately. And when challenged, Jesus said, 'A more important issue than the Temple is here.'

The law was made to bring us to God, not to make us puffed-up, self-righteous snobs who were so busy not being wrong that we forget how to love. *A more important issue than the Temple is here.*

The Sabbath was made so that we could worship, so that we could rest, so that we could enjoy time off work. It was not made to be a burden. *A more important issue than the Temple is here.*

When Jesus plucked the ears of corn and ate on the Sabbath he was also making a statement about food. Food is for people; it is not for profit. Food is for the hungry; it is not for stock piling. Food is for eating; it is not for wasting. *A more important issue than the Temple is here.*

This building is beautiful. It is for using and enjoying and being the place where we worship. It is also for sharing with the community and parish. *But it is not to be worshipped.* It is a building. Let no-one worship the building or make this church an idol. For that is spiritual death. Jesus has liberated us from that enslavement.

In the letter of Peter we read that we are the living stones: come let yourselves be built as living stones into a spiritual temple.

When we leave this church, people will not judge Christianity or the claims of Jesus by the painting of the building. Outsiders will judge Christianity and the claims of Christ by our daily living. It is the simple gifts of the spirit, simple but so hard, which show the living Christ – generosity and kindness, a willingness to share in others' joys and sorrows, a listening ear, a smiling welcome, a kindly word. These all speak of Christ and a spiritual life. For although the stones of the kirk matter, it is the living stones of the people that matter more. When we leave this building, we become the church. Come let *us* be built as living stones into a spiritual temple.

NOTE

1. Scottish Psalter, Psalm 102, ii, v. 14.

12

Heavenly Tasting

A COMMUNION SERMON

Readings:	*Genesis 1:24–31*
	Colossians 1:15–20
	Luke 22:14–20
Occasion:	**Communion Service**

Last Sunday evening, my husband and I were invited out to a meal. It was a precise invitation: 'Come at 7 p.m. to help us eat a fish.' The fish, which turned out to be an enormous salmon, had been caught by a friend in the River Cassley on the boundary between Sutherland and Easter Ross. Our friend was quite happy to admit that he had fished there for several years and had never before caught anything. So he and his wife asked us to come to celebrate, and to help them to eat the fish. And as we were getting ready, I said to my husband, the way one does,

- 'What should we wear?'
- 'How many people will be there?'
- 'Will it be sit down or buffet?'
- 'Do you think I'll know anyone?'

And he answered, as husbands do, 'I have no idea.' An invitation to a dinner party or a night out is special for all of us. It is an occasion. Usually we try to be punctual, suitably dressed, make an effort at conversation and generally behave well. We may even take a wee pressie and if very well mannered may write a note of thanks afterwards. This is all part of the ritual of being invited out to a party.

Today, we share another meal that has rituals built around it. Some of the rituals come from the Bible, from Jesus. Some of them come from history or tradition. Some of them come from this country and this culture.

I hope that everyone here enjoys the meal. I hope everyone has come because they want to come. I hope no-one is worried about what they are wearing, although I confess to a liking for bright and colourful clothes rather than sombre and dark clothes. I hope that no-one is worried about how to behave. The truth is that although it is a meal and a shared meal, it is not that sort of meal. It is a celebration of Christian belief and faith. It is a sharing in the death and life of Christ. It is placing ourselves in that history.

Let me read you something:

Three-year-old Timothy had just heard his mother read his favourite bedtime story for the third time. After the third and final reading, his mother witnessed a strange phenomenon. The little boy took the book and set it on the ground. Then he opened the book, gently put one foot and then the other on the open pages, and looked down in wonderment and then began to cry. The mother was quite puzzled at this little display until her eight-year-old daughter offered this simple interpretation: 'Timmy really likes the book'. It was then that the mother understood: Timothy wanted to become part of the story.[1]

The story of this meal begins in creation and takes us to heaven. We move from slavery to a promised land. We pass from exile to freedom. We look into a stable and hear angel voices. We see a child running on the shore at Galilee and arguing with his mother.

We hear snatches of stories and listen to riddles. We hear laughter and weeping, questions and arguments. And there were plenty of shared meals, but one special one. It started as a meal like so many, but became different. 'For you,' he said, 'for you.' 'My body for you.' We hide our eyes from the hardness a cross. Switch it off and make a cup of tea. But we have to watch the three long hours, the three long days. 'Forgive them.' 'Forgive them.' 'It is finished.'

But it wasn't and it isn't, for the voice was there again, and the call came again, 'Feed my lambs.' 'Come and eat.'

For that unknown man, in that small country, in that distant time, was the God of heaven and earth, lifting us from earth to heaven in a meal of bread and wine.

Today, we stand on the book. We become part of the story. We insert our feet on to the page with so many from different centuries and countries. It matters not what we wear or what we look like or what we earn or even if we understand. If we want to be part of the story, that is enough.

Wherever people meet to share bread or wine in the name of Jesus Christ, incarnate, crucified, risen, they become part of the story. They may be Lutherans in Scandinavia. They may be Anglicans in England. They may be members of a United Church – as in India or Canada or Australia. They may be Roman Catholics in Italy or the Philippines. They may be like us, part of the Reformed family. And we can find members of the Reformed or Presbyterian family in Scotland or Hungary or Switzerland or many countries in Africa and around the world.

In most Christian churches there is a prayer which asks God to bless the gifts of bread and wine:

> Send down your Holy Spirit
> to bless us
> and these your gifts of bread and wine,

that the bread which we break
may be for us the communion
of the body of Christ,
and the cup of blessing which we bless
the communion of the blood of Christ.[2]

There is the feeling that we wait with open arms and hearts and call God down. Today, however, the prayer we shall use is different. It is part of the Scottish story as well as part of the great Christian story. It comes from Calvin's Geneva, via John Knox and the Scottish reformers of the sixteenth century.

Here, we declare
and witness before the world that,
by him alone we have received liberty and life,
by him alone you claim us as children and heirs,
by him alone we have access to your favour, freely shown,
by him alone we are raised
into your spiritual kingdom,
there to eat and drink with you and the Son
at that most joyful table of eternal life.[3]

As we rejoice in our full redemption and raise our hearts to God, so we, on this earth, are raised to heaven itself for a sweet foretaste of eternal joy.

In this present time,
we on earth have communion *with you in heaven.*
But in the time to come,
we shall be raised to that endless joy,
prepared for us before the foundation
of the world was laid.[4]

Today, we set our feet on the story. Today, we shall be raised with those whom we have loved and lost. We shall be raised with

Knox and Calvin, with Peter and Andrew, with Mary and Mary Magdalene, with Abraham and Isaac and Jacob, raised into the spiritual Kingdom there to eat and drink with God ... We *on earth* have communion in heaven. But in the time to come we shall be raised to that endless joy, prepared for us before the foundation of the world was laid.

NOTES

1. Herbert Anderson and Edward Foley, *Mighty Stories, Dangerous Rituals* (San Francisco: Jossey-Bass Publishers, 1998), p. 27.
2. *Common Order* (Edinburgh: Saint Andrew Press, 1994), p. 133.
3. Ibid., p. 135.
4. Ibid.

13

The Kingdom of the Absent King

A STORY ABOUT THE CHURCH

Readings:	*Psalm 105:1–11*
	Romans 8:31–9
	Matthew 13:31–5
Season:	*Seventh Sunday after Pentecost*

One evening last week, I fell asleep in the sun and had a dream. I'd like to tell you about it. So, are you sitting comfortably? Then I'll begin.

Once upon a time there was a young king. He was good and he was godly. He loved his people and spent much time with them. He spent a lot of time talking to people. He didn't say anything new, except one thing (we'll come to that later), but he said things in such a nice way, mainly by telling stories, that people loved him. Also, he lived what he taught, so people who had never really thought much began to understand what love and life were all about, and they began to be really, really happy. He spent little time or money on himself, but shared what he had, and enjoyed life as a God-given gift. He did not marry, which caused his mother some concern, and she was always trying to arrange for him to meet a nice girl (I think she wanted grandchildren), but to no avail. Because he was a man of such goodness, he was greatly loved by his own people. And when he told them that he would be travelling very far away, and taking no-one with him, some of his people became anxious for his safety and for theirs.

However, he made them some promises:

- I'll be with you in spirit.
- I shall come back to you.
- I am preparing a place for you.

And he gave them some commands (being a king he could do that):

- Tell everyone about me.
- Love everyone else as much as you love yourself.
- Love your enemies (that was the one really new thing that he told people).

He gave them words of comfort:

- I'll be with you till the end of time.
- My peace I leave with you, not any old peace, but mine.

And he left them with a challenge:

- As my father sent me, so I send you.
- I hold you accountable to me.

And then he went away. In fact, he was killed. Astonishingly, the story tells us that he kept coming back, as though he couldn't bear to leave them, and he kept on giving extra little messages to his closest friends. The friends included men and women, rich and poor, trades people and professional folk from all shades of political opinions. But, finally, he did go.

And the people who had really liked him rushed around like mad. They kept telling strangers how wonderful he was and how others should follow this way of life, too. They worked hard at trying to keep the memory true. It was difficult because they didn't know where he was. Some eventually decided that they should write down some of the sayings, some of the teaching. And, eventually, some thought it might be good to write down what some of the great events of his life had been – a sort of biography. And they gathered regularly to go over the memory, especially to share a meal together, a meal which became the most important part of the memory work.

And what happened after all that?

It was quite amazing really, because the young king did not come back. And many, many of his followers were most cruelly treated and killed in frenzied and bloody attacks.

So, of course, if this had been a fairy story, everything would have died the death. But this is not a fairy story, as you well know.

The movement, the group that believed in him, the followers of the way, gathered momentum. There was at one level a teasing, thoughtful quality to his way of life. It was totally different from any world movement or philosophy that had gone before. If only one had the courage to try it! On the other hand it was so supremely simple – to do with being loved and forgiven and accepted. So it appealed to the poor and the illiterate and the peasants and simple folk. And it also appealed to humble intellectuals (it was said there were some around when he was a baby), and courageous criminals, and honest business folk, and people who had no self-respect left.

Broadly speaking, the bumptious and arrogant and self-made and judgemental did not find it enticing – except for one or two strange stories. About a stuck-up so-and-so who did a lot of damage in the early days. He was stopped in his tracks one day and ended up embracing the whole thing – hook, line and sinker!

People who had been the king's closest friends started to die or were killed off, so the writings became even more important. And they were copied laboriously by hand and travelled around all sorts of places. They were used so much at meetings and rolled and unrolled that bits began to fall off them and more copies were made and little mistakes crept in and people added comments or explanations and they got copied, too. Then folk who had known him dictated their memories – for example, his mother spoke to an awfully nice young doctor who could write beautifully, and he wrote down quite a lot of interesting things. The written things were copied and edited and put together and they became even more important than the letters that people had started to write and send to new groups.

The Kingdom of the absent king extended overseas, first to places in the middle east, then to Africa, to the country called Ethiopia, to Asia, to the Indian subcontinent, also to Mediterranean Europe and eventually all over the known world.

The followers had three things to go by, and these are important, so mark them, they are still the only things that the followers have:

- the written word;
- the tradition handed down;
- the inner leading and the inner light.

The followers argued and made up. The followers argued and split up. Sometimes they talked and sometimes they fought. But always they tried, in their own way, to listen to the promises, and the commands, and the comfort and the challenge.

Then there came a bad time, a time when other ways beckoned. The nations of the world were often at war. There was much money and much poverty. There was great comfort and great pain. People became materialistic and lived selfish lives. Others lived good lives in a secular way. And the believers' children drifted away. And every now and again, the followers of the king say, with varying degrees of self-pity:

- 'What am I doing here?'
- 'How can we best serve the king nowadays?'
- 'The whole culture has changed.'
- 'We should set up a commission.'
- 'Why are we doing all the work?'
- 'I am the only one who cares.'
- 'We should employ a youth worker.'
- 'There's so much apathy around, not like when I was young.'

Then suddenly I heard an anguished cry and a voice saying: 'Father, forgive them, they don't know what they are doing.'

Then the voice said, 'Whenever you give bread to the hungry, clothe the naked, visit the sick or those in prison, give water to the thirsty, you do it to me.'

'You are the yeast. Only yeast. But let the yeast work.'

Then another voice said, 'His followers have never stopped worshipping and serving. Think of the schools and hospitals throughout the world which have been started and staffed in his name. Think of the mental hospitals and the schools for children with disabilities that were all started in his name. Think of the food distributed, homeless housed, refugees welcomed and prisoners freed in his name. His followers have been at the frontiers in caring for people with leprosy or AIDS. They have spearheaded the movement to cancel unrepayable debt. No age has been left without his faithful servants. And they are still at it, with faithful prayer, with courageous witness, generosity unbounded and with hope unquenched. Do not wring your hands about the apathy of others.'

Still follow the man hanging on the cross who cries with pain and then says, 'Forgive them, they don't know what they are doing.' For he is your challenge, your comfort, your hope, your promise, your command. The absent king will return. Meanwhile, possess the Kingdom.

There *is* no ending to this story – yet. The next chapter in the story of the church is yours.

14

The Great Stone Ship

THE CHURCH AS CRUSADE AND SANCTUARY

Readings:	*Psalm 27:1–6, 13–14*
	Acts 28:11–15
	Matthew 21:10–17
Season:	*Ninth Sunday after Pentecost*

When the Abbey of the Holy Rood in Edinburgh was founded by David I in the twelfth century it became a sanctuary. The ruins of the Abbey still stand within the grounds of the Palace of Holyrood House. If you have never stood there and marvelled at your own history, try it one sunny morning. The centuries close in around you, and it is not impossibly hard to believe that you can see the strange mixture of petty thieves, debtors, the deranged or murderers, who would seek asylum and sanctuary amidst the monks and priests from those who would harass and punish them. The practice carried on long past the Reformation well into the eighteenth century, although by that time, with the establishment of modern law and some sort of understanding of illness, sanctuary would be mainly for debtors. But for long enough, it was a place of sanctuary.

- A place of refuge.
- A place of security.

- A place of peace, of safety, of asylum.
- A safe haven in a storm.
- Somewhere to curl up and hide.
- Somewhere to allow yourself to be fragile or vulnerable or different.

The three readings can guide our thoughts.

1. The reading from the book of Psalms is a most wonderful expression of God's house as a place of safety.

We don't know what the writer was frightened of – perhaps enemies with spears and swords? People who were going to kill him with hatred and lies? People who were jealous or ambitious or insecure? Or were the terrors from within – searing loneliness, depression beyond imagining, life-stopping inadequacy? Whoever or whatever they were, the writer was terrified to death. It was the sort of terror and paralysing fear that comes during an air raid if your city is being bombed. It is the cold and numb fear when someone you love is having an operation that could be life saving but is life threatening. It is the fear of death that grips this man. And in the middle of it, he is able to say: *The Lord is my light and my salvation; whom should I fear? ... He will keep me safe beneath his roof in the day of misfortune.* Isn't that a lovely line? *He will keep me safe beneath his roof in the day of misfortune.*

This church building is made of stone. But the church is more than stone; it is a community of people. Nevertheless the building is important. That is why we lavish so much money and thought and care on it. That is why we plan, and plan, and plan for the next generation. Sometimes I wish we lived in a world of greater trust where we could leave these doors open so that anyone, throughout the daylight hours at least, anyone who wanted to, could come into this place to sit, to pray, to feel the peace of it seep into their very bones and soul.

I do not know what hurt you are nursing. I do not know what pain or fear or emptiness grips you. I do believe that here, within God's house, you may be able to find the assurance you seek. *The Lord is my light and my salvation; whom should I fear? . . . He will keep me safe beneath his roof in the day of misfortune.*

This place is a sanctuary – a place of peace for those who are hurting and seek solace. This sanctuary is for you.

2. The gospel reading reminds us that the Temple, according to Jesus, was a place of prayer for all nations. It was or should have been a place where anyone could go who was looking for God. But there were those who made money out of it all, and became rich by preying on the faithful poor. This is one of the few parts of the gospel where we read that Jesus became really angry. He was angry because the people who should have enabled the seekers and the faithful to come were making it hard for them. There should be room for everyone – the least and the last and the lost. No-one should make it hard for a person to come to church, and sometimes we do. No-one should put up barriers to prevent people coming here, but sometimes we do. We may not mean to, but by concentrating on our own little groups of friends to whom we must have a blether, we may exclude the stranger or visitor or the person who is hurting. Even our very obvious friendship with one another may appear to be exclusive and excluding. This place must have a quality of universality about it. It is God's house, not ours.

3. The reading from the book of Acts is one of the first instances of the church in action with all its many races and many cultures. In general, when you read the Old Testament, you see a people trying to purify themselves and keep to strict rules. They were trying to keep themselves apart. There were times when no-one

was allowed to marry an outsider. Any sort of diversity was regarded as 'un-Jewish'.

In these few verses from the book of Acts, Paul, on his way to Rome to be imprisoned first, and then executed, meets fellow Christians wherever he is, Christians whom he had never met before. People who were totally unknown to him came to meet him. Finally, he arrives in the capital city of that great empire that occupied almost the entire known world. Listen to the understated writing:

> And so to Rome. The Christians there had had news of us and came out to meet us as far as the Appian Forum and the Three Inns. And when Paul saw them, he gave thanks to God and took courage.

Paul, remember, was under armed guard and was being escorted to Rome to stand trial. They had been shipwrecked and had spent the winter in Malta. They then took this large merchant vessel and, crossing the sea, landed briefly at Sicily. From there they travelled to mainland Italy, touching the west toe of the country in the town that is now called Reggio di Calabria. A south wind brought them to what is now Pozzuoli, at that time a large grain port. From there they travelled by road. Forty-three miles from Rome they were met by a Christian delegation. It would have been easy for any Christians in Rome to have gone indoors and found something else to do. But in fact word went around and the Christian community came out to meet him. Ten miles further in at the Three Inns, a second group was waiting. Were they standing in silence? Or did they have large placards saying: 'We're rooting for Paul'? I simply do not know. But Paul recognised that they were the church in the place. He recognised that they had come to be seen publicly. And suddenly he was not alone. *And when Paul saw them, he gave thanks to God and took courage.*

The church is a gathering of people as well as a building. In this case, *the church came out to give sanctuary* to Paul. They could not offer the security of the building. But they could offer the fellowship of faith and of prayer. And they did. *And when Paul saw them, he gave thanks to God and took courage.*

The old Soviet Union used to have Youth Festivals, which were large propaganda exercises. My husband went to one in 1956 as part of the Christian delegation. All of them decided that they would wear crosses on their lapels. Because there were so many there, it was easy to escape from the constant surveillance, and one day he and a friend wandered off into the streets of Moscow. While looking at the shops and the meagre merchandise, an old woman accosted them. She was tiny and shrivelled and had lines, furrows, on her face as of centuries of suffering. She was dressed in black and had a black head scarf over her head. In her hand she carried a few vegetables. But she shook their sleeves and made them stop and pointed to their crosses. Then from inside her dress she pulled a cross which she reverently kissed before disappearing back into the crowd. Perhaps like Paul, *when she saw them, she gave thanks to God and took courage.*

The church is a sanctuary for those who look for peace or rescue or deliverance or for space. Whether in a building or whether in a group of people that is still true.

I started this sermon with the image of Holy Rood Abbey as a sanctuary. In closing, let me leave you with another picture. St Magnus Cathedral in Orkney is a small cathedral as cathedrals go. It nestles in Kirkwall, solid, secure, foursquare against the fierce winds and storms of the north. It was built during a time when the flower of the people and the bulk of the money was being spent on crusades to the Holy Land, a crusade that was stained with blood and robbery and persecution of the Muslims. It was marked by death and disaster, by stolen gold and storms, sunken ships and warfare. The saga of the crusade was celebrated a few years ago in the most stunning display of banners and paintings and poetry within the cathedral. The very last word was given by George Mackay Brown. And this is what he wrote:

> So ended the most famous recorded voyage that the Orkneymen ever made.
>
> . . . While the Crusaders were on their famous voyage, slowly in Orkney the walls of St Magnus Cathedral were rising, the great stone ship that was to bear the people of Orkney through many generations.[1]

St Magnus Cathedral is a sanctuary – a great stone ship. And so is St Michael's for us – the building and the people. May it also be, under God, a place of safety and healing and help for us and for generations still to come.

NOTE

1. George Mackay Brown, from *Sails in St Magnus*, the brochure produced for the exhibition in 1993.

A Touching Place – Jesus

15

Saying and Doing

LENT

Readings:	*Genesis 17:1–8, 15–22*
	Mark 8:27–38
Season:	*Second Sunday in Lent*

I have discovered an e-mail from heaven specially for us. This is what it says:

To:

allsaints@stmichaels.co.edinburgh.scotland

From:

mark@saintsalive.cloudnine.seventhheaven.co.eternity

Grace to you and peace from the Lord Jesus Christ.

My dear friends, it was good to be in touch with you. Such a relief that it is now possible to communicate with people direct. Before it was so difficult always to be receiving anguished prayers from saints on earth and to suffer the frustration of knowing that very rarely would they listen for a reply. Oh dear! All those long prayers that start, 'We do just ask you for . . .' And would they take the time to be quiet and listen for the reply? You will have gathered that we saints sometimes became quite impatient even in heaven!

Anyway, I was saying how good it is to be in touch with folk who really want to know about those times in Galilee with the Master. You were asking about his great call to discipleship. The first call was early on and evidently my cousins, Andrew and Peter and co., just said 'Yes' without knowing what they were doing. And then there was this second great call to follow. It was much harder that time. Those around him were still not opening their eyes. They were quite blind to what was going on. That's why, when much later on I wrote everything down, I told the story of the blind man who was cured immediately before I told about this. And the next miracle was of the boy who was deaf – I was trying to make the point that we were all a bit blind and deaf.

Well, we were just coming up towards Caesarea and suddenly Jesus turns to Peter, that's my cousin Peter, and says, 'Well then, you can tell me now, what are people saying about me? Everything depends on who people think I am. So who do people say that I am?' The way he spoke it was in capital letters. WHO DO PEOPLE SAY THAT I AM?

They all looked at each other with those sideways looks, as if to say, 'Go on, you speak first.' Then John said, as though distancing himself from the reply in case it was wrong, 'Some people say you are John the Baptist.' Matthew said, 'Others think you might be Elijah.' But then Matthew wanted to believe that because Elijah had to come back again before the Messiah comes in his glory.

The Messiah in glory. *That* will be the day we have been waiting for – a huge magnificent D-day. We could hardly wait for it. Blood and terror all round we reckoned. Death for the Romans and glory for us – and for God, too, of course.

So Jesus looks at us as if to say: 'Is that all you can say?' I remember it well because at that time Jesus stopped walking. I had been running along trying to listen to what they were saying which is always hard when you are behind the people, and Jesus stopped so suddenly that I banged into him. He wasn't angry, though I think he hadn't known I was there. He turned and grinned at me. Then he put his hand on Peter's shoulder and said, 'And you, my friend, who do *you* say that I am?' And Peter did that little stammer he sometimes did when he got excited and said, 'You're the M-m-messiah.' 'Right,' said Jesus, and he looked kind of pleased. Then he said, 'Don't you dare say a word about this.'

So that's what happened.

Then he told us the stuff about suffering. All our dreams of D-day suddenly crashed and we hated him. We wanted those no-good Romans turfed out of *our* country. And we wanted those bastard traitor collaborators to be shown up for what they were before public execution. We would gladly have cheered as they were nailed to their rotten crosses. Then the Messiah would come in glory and we would be right there in the front row . . . We couldn't wait.

Then Jesus told us things we didn't want to hear. I remember Judas Iscariot, he was always nice to me was Judas, he put his fingers in his ears. And Philip covered his eyes. We couldn't believe what he said. Thomas stared and stared as if Jesus was speaking in a foreign language.

- Suffering.
- Rejection.
- Death.

It was a horrible moment. Suffering? Rejection? Death? It was as though the sun had gone in.

Peter couldn't bear it any longer. He started forward and shook Jesus hard. 'What are you saying? Don't be so stupid. You're a huge success. Everyone loves you. You'll take Jerusalem by storm. You'll . . .'

Well, Jesus turned on all of us and quelled the lot of us with one look. Then he turned on Peter, on *Peter*! 'Hold your tongue,' he said. 'You don't know what sort of damage you can do.' Peter was set to argue but Jesus got really angry, 'Don't "but" me. Get behind me, you Satan, you. You're still thinking like all the others. Listen to God. Hear God. You're so blind. So deaf. You're so stupid.' He was shaking. And we didn't know what to do.

We went on walking and reached Caesarea Philippi. A crowd gathered and he encouraged it for once, and then he talked about self-denial.

We were all a bit embarrassed for a while. Jesus seemed sad that we couldn't understand. He kept muttering about having ears and not hearing, having eyes and not seeing. Then Peter said that we may not be able to see and we may not be able to hear but we were able to smell and we did, not because we had noses, but because we needed a bath. And Jesus laughed like anything and we all stripped and had a swim and felt better about things.

Long, long after I puzzled about the self-denial bit.

Jesus never asked us to be less than true to ourselves. Jesus always wanted us to find out who we were, what we were good at, what we wanted to do. Jesus wanted us to be the best we could be.

- He was the greatest encourager I have ever known.
- He could see good in us that no-one else could see.
- He made greedy people generous.
- He was able to persuade shy people to speak in public.
- He put a child in the centre of things.
- He would talk to old beggars.

- He touched people with leprosy.
- He let a prostitute wash his feet.
- He spoke to Romans and was kind to them.
- He treated women as equals.

We thought that was a mistake at first but he had the last laugh because instead of showing himself after his resurrection to two Jewish men, which is the only reliable witness in a Jewish court, he showed himself to *one woman* – and she was a tart! So he was serious about equality.

He drew out the absolute best in everyone he met. He wanted people to be the best that they could be. He wanted people to dance and sing and fly through the world, to shine like stars and to exult in God's creation and cry, 'Glory! Glory! Glory to God!'

Denial? Denial is not about rejecting who you really are or about pretending to be holy. Denial is about *knowing* who you are, *enjoying* who you are, *embracing* this life with its gifts and pain and creativity and its possibilities, and saying, 'Blessed Jesus, this is who I am, thank you for that. And all that I am is for you.'

With hindsight, I think Jesus was speaking to particular sections of the community.

- To Jews rather than foreigners,
- to men rather than women,
- to the bosses rather than to servants,
- to the educated rather than the uneducated,
- to the upper classes rather than the lower classes,
- to the superior (so-called) races rather than the despised races,
- to the rich rather than the poor.

I do feel that now, because refugees, women, slaves, un-educated, working classes, blacks and the poor are people who know all about self-denial. Society has made them deny themselves. They always believe that the business of other people is more important than their own.

I think Jesus was talking to the rich and the powerful, to the religious and political rulers, to the educated wealthy boss people, mainly men.

And yet, he was speaking to everyone. For we all have within us the capacity to shine for Christ. And the capacity to turn in upon ourselves. Self-denial – give up sweets or alcohol if you want. True self-denial is about shining for Christ, living for Christ, giving for Christ and loving for Christ.

And when we are totally centred on Christ, if we ever can be, then we truly find ourselves.

My dear friends, I have wearied you with my anecdotes and my memories. But it's such a pleasure to be able to share these memories of my Galilean youth, memories still sharp and sweet and clear.

From your dear friend and colleague in Christ, Mark. And to God be the glory.

16

The Women Who Stayed

GOOD FRIDAY

These are short meditations on people who are on the margin of the passion story. They were started in 1998 for the end of the Churches' Decade of Solidarity with Women and were added to over the years, both in Toorak Uniting Church, Melbourne, and in St Michael's, Edinburgh.

THE SERVING WOMAN WITHOUT A NAME

> *Reading:*   *Luke 22:54–61*

I worked for a while as a maid at the house of Caiaphas. He was the high priest. The work was hard, but there was always plenty to eat and that wasn't true of all the big houses. Some I know were so careful with food there was never extra for the servants. Many a time in other jobs I went to bed hungry. But the high priest was good that way. Besides, it was an interesting place to work. There was always something going on and you saw some strange folk.

There was one day in particular that I shall never forget. That was the day, or rather the night, that they brought in Jesus of Nazareth – a joiner he was from the hill country of the Galilee.

There was something about him that was, well, it was different. I mean, he wasn't a criminal – I've seen them. If they are arrested they are either drunk and truculent or they are whimpering and whingeing, blaming everyone else. Sometimes they are madly desperately violent – ready to fight for whatever cause they think they have. This man wasn't any of these things. He just stood there, all quiet and dignified for all the world like a young prince. And he wasn't like the lawyers and scribes who would call to see the high priest professionally and stay and have a drink and a meal. He was different. He was so ordinary, and yet superior if you get my meaning.

Anyway, it got up the nose of the guard and they started having fun with him – you know, goading him and laughing and pushing him and of course it got out of control. It became rough, nasty, cruel. And he took it. Not in a cringing way – but just took it, like old cotton waste mopping up spilled blood.

Friends of his had come in with him. They hung around at the back. I saw them from the first. It's my job to see who comes and goes in the courtyard. One of them was quite pushy. He got right up by the fire and all the time he couldn't take his eyes off this Jesus. I expected him to go up closer to show a bit of support. So I leaned over and said to him: 'You were with him, weren't you?' He jumped like the cat caught with his face in the cream jug! 'I was not,' he said. 'I've never seen him in my life.' I knew he was lying. I'd only interfered to help, not to accuse. So I busied myself getting more wood and filling their glasses. Later on someone else asked the same. And an hour or so later a third person noticed him. The man still claimed that he didn't know Jesus, but he never stopped looking at him.

And then Jesus slowly turned. He had a gash over his eye, and blood was trickling down the side of his mouth from a punch he had had. And he looked at this man, his friend . . . My God, I hope no-one ever looks at me like that. It wasn't anger. It was more like, 'Don't leave me alone.' It reminded me of the time I had to put my little girl to board with another family while I went out to work.

Anyway, by that time it was morning. The cock had been crowing fit to burst. I went to get the hens' feed ready. What a night.

PILATE'S WIFE

Pilate's wife is another nameless woman. The crime novelist Dorothy Sayers wrote a famous set of radio plays called Man Born to be King, *and she called Pilate's wife Claudia Procula. So I shall call her that, too.*

Reading: *Matthew 27:11–26*

My name is Claudia. I am a Roman and I am of noble birth. My husband was appointed to Jerusalem – about as far east as you can get in the Roman Empire. Odd that, because he was born in a corner of the empire as far north and as far west as you can get, in a Godforsaken country called Scotland. Anyway, like many wives forced into colonial exile by their husbands' jobs, time used to hang heavily on my hands. There was, of course, the official entertaining. But the servants did the work. It was all on expenses. I just gave the orders and it was done. The roasted meats, the wines, the spices, the breads, the cheeses, the honey, the wonderful fruit, the sweetmeats. There was nothing for me to do except keep myself beautiful and smile on the men that my husband had to impress.

I wasn't allowed to fraternise with the natives, but in spite of the rules of diplomatic protocol, I was drawn to these people, these strange and beautiful people, the Jews. The religious ones have such certainty. Their morality was so clear cut. Their laws so plain. They had an uncanny pride – I don't mean arrogance. I mean a real sense that they belonged and that we were the temporary residents. I began to feel uncomfortable that I was in their country. It didn't seem right somehow. There was no justice in it. Justice – now that was something that my husband knew about. He was always being called to give judgement on someone or another.

I never interfered until one day. That Day. Ever since, it has been a watershed in my life. I wakened after a bad night. I had had such dreams – terrible, horrible, frightening dreams! And they were all to do with this man up from the country called Jesus. I recognised him, although I wouldn't tell my husband *that.* I had sneaked out of the palace with one of my maids months before and had heard Jesus speaking. The laughter and love in his voice I remember so clearly. 'Happy are the merciful,' he had said. Mercy was scarcely a word that was known in the Roman administration. We always feel we have to punish to make an example. 'Happy are the peacemakers.' How can you be happy letting foreigners take over the country? 'Happy are the poor.' The poor? Happy are the *poor*? A couple of times we managed to hear him. There was something so special about him. He said he would never turn anyone away. His voice was full of tenderness and laughter and strength all at once. He made me feel good about myself. And he spoke about God as if there were only one God, and as if he *knew* him really well. One day he spoke about carrying a cross and it sent shivers down my spine.

That morning I wakened with the nightmares and these awful dreams still going round my head. Then I discovered that Pilate was to make a judgement on this man, Jesus. So I, Claudia, begged my husband to have nothing to do with this man of innocence. But he wouldn't listen. My husband Pilate gave his judgement and washed his hands in public. I cried that night. He told me not to worry my pretty little head about things I didn't understand. The whole thing will be forgotten in a fortnight.

Forgotten in a fortnight? That was forty years ago. My husband is long dead. I live in Rome and I am a follower of The Way. We meet once a week to break bread. And sometimes we say together, 'I believe in Jesus, Lord, suffered under Pontius Pilate, crucified, dead and buried. The third day he rose from the dead.'

THE WEEPING WOMEN

> *Reading:*   *Luke 23:26–34*

My name is Rebecca. I am one of the weeping women of Jerusalem. It is our job to follow funerals and cry. We've seen plenty of crucifixions, I can tell you, but this one was different. We followed him out of the city – some of us had followed him before and heard him speak. He had a strange power. We watched him stagger until they got some poor foreigner to help him carry his cross. Funny. The one time I had heard him, he had said that there would be a cross to carry. I thought he had meant a cross inside. Like a baby. But this was real enough.

Anyway, he was going to die sure enough, so we started on the funeral hymns and dirges. And he stopped dead. He turned and looked at us and said:

Dry your eyes. Put away your tears. Don't cry for me but for yourselves and for your own children.

101

And, just for a minute, I thought I saw what he meant. This sort of cruelty and viciousness doesn't end when the poor fellow is strung up there on the cross. It breeds. So the one who gave the judgement and the ones who hammer the nails and we women who keen away while we're thinking of what we'll make for supper tonight are all part of it. It has to stop or else we destroy ourselves and our children. But how?

And then I looked again, and I saw him perhaps for the first time. It *can* stop now. With him. On the cross. I started to cry again. But this time my tears were real. Because I had helped to put him here and he's taking the blame. Taking it all. Up there on the cross.

MARY, THE MOTHER

> *Reading:*   *John 19:23–30*

I am Mary, mother of Jesus, this man on the cross. I loved him, always, but I did not always understand him. He was such a lovely child. Always asking questions, not just for the sake of asking as some children do, but because he was interested. He would listen to the answer so carefully. The same with Joseph in the shop. 'Why do you spend so long smoothing that bit of wood, Dad?' 'Is it so the yoke is comfy?' He was difficult as a teenager. But what child is not? He ran away once, the rascal. What a row we gave him. Even then it was different – not with a girl and not with the best wine skin, but to the Temple, if you please. It made it hard to be angry, but when we got back home he got it hot and strong.

Why did he not marry and give me grandchildren? Why did he have to leave home with his friends? I know they were nice enough men, from good honest God-fearing homes, most of them. But I sometimes found it hard to be civil to them. They took him away from me. Why did he sometimes, no, often, put loyalty to them above loyalty to me? Did he ever know how hurt I was by it all? Why did he talk about sharing his heavenly Father with everyone? And now they, who sucked the life blood from him, have run away – all save young John. Friends he called them. Some friends!

But he is mine and I am his. We are together again, he and I. I never understood his obsession with sharing his love with everyone. As I said, I did not always understand him. But, in a terrible way, I understand this better. It reminds me of that time in Bethlehem. I felt alone then. Alone to bear the pain and the fear and the disgrace. I nearly gave up. And then he was born. And he was beautiful. I know all mothers say that. But he *was* beautiful. And I held him close and knew that he was my destiny. Joseph was so kind. Doing his loving and slightly clumsy best. But the child, my son, lay in my arms and I felt like bursting with joy at the wonder of it. Where did I go wrong? Was I too strict? Were we not strict enough?

I want to hold him close again. Once again to wash away blood with my tears. To cradle his head in my arms. To cover his nakedness and wrap him in my best cloth. That time at Bethlehem, I felt I had the whole world in my arms. I wish I could give birth to him again. That pain was worth it. But this pain . . . does it accomplish anything?

MARY OF MAGDALA

We don't know a huge amount about Mary of Magdala, although there are many stories about her. It is thought she may have been a prostitute. One thing every gospel tells us is that a company of women stayed to the end at the foot of the cross. The only one named in all *the gospels is Mary of Magdala. It was to her that the message of evangelism was committed by the risen Christ: go and tell. She was, indeed, the Apostle to the Apostles.*

Reading: Mark 15:40–1

I was there. It would have been impossible for me to leave. A whole gang of us women were around him. We cooked, and we washed their clothes, and we followed him around. Some of the women with younger children could be there only for a short time. If he came to Capernaum, all the mums there would be out like a shot. He was so good to be with. But then when he moved on they couldn't follow. It was the same in every town we went to. Some women were there most of the time. His mother. She was a real good soul. And then there was that jumped up jack-in-the-box Mrs Zebedee, who thought her precious sons were better than the rest and she asked for them to sit beside him when he comes in glory. Huh. Fat chance!

I had no children. At least none that I could name and show as mine. So I was able to be there right to the end. It was going to be wonderful because he would surprise us all. I knew he would – he was always doing the opposite of what people expected. For example when his friends tried to chase away some children, he scolded his friends and brought the children back and played with them and blessed them. When people thought we were all going to starve that time, he fed us all with practically nothing. When the wine ran out at a wedding, he produced more. When he touched a man with leprosy we thought he would catch the disease, but it was the man with leprosy who caught good health. When those fishermen caught nothing all night, as soon as Jesus appeared they caught masses of fish.

So you see I knew it would be all right in the end. All those so-called disciples running away. Call themselves friends? I despised them just as they despised me. After all it's men like them that make women like me what we are. But I *knew* that it would be all right. He would transform everything. He would wait till the end and then everyone would bow before him and it would be wonderful. So, yes, I followed him right to the cross. Even with the flogging and the beatings he had had, I was *sure* it would work out.

'Trust me,' he used to say. 'You can start a new life. You can live a new wonderful life full of real love, not this sham stuff.' When I was with him, I could do it. And he made the others accept me, although it was touch and go with some of them. Once a whore always a whore – that's what they said behind my back. But he used to say, 'Mary, my friend, in my Father's kingdom, it will be love, real love, that matters – and you have plenty of that. Respect yourself more.' He was wonderful.

So, yes, I followed him right to the cross. I watched waiting for the miracle through my tears. But it didn't happen. He was in such pain – real terrible agonising pain. He could hardly breathe and he kept pushing himself up on the cross to get a bit of air. And you could hear the blood and water gurgling in his lungs as he choked to death. He shouted out a couple of times. He gasped a few words to his mother and to John. He went delirious for a while and muttered a bit of a psalm. And then he screamed out and he died. And the miracle hadn't happened.

I hated God. I hated him. Hated him. How could he let Jesus down. Up there in his beautiful heaven, so far away from us. So I thought to myself that if God wouldn't help him, I would do it myself. It's the last thing I can do for him. They took him down and I saw that this guy with money had bought him in some way, so I followed, with some of the other women. And we noted the *exact spot* where he had been shoved into the tomb. I was itching to wash him, to wash his matted hair and blood-soaked body, and put his best clean white shirt on. We saw exactly where he was and we planned to go as soon as the Sabbath was over.

God. You can keep him. I'll never believe again. Jesus was the only one who has ever loved me. If God can do this to him . . . I hate him. But I'll be there on Sunday morning. As soon as the sun is up, I'll be there. You can count on me, Jesus.

17

Change of Life

EASTER

Readings:	Acts 10:34–43
	1 Corinthians 15:1–11
	Mark 16:1–8
Season:	Easter Day. This sermon is the second half of the meditation on Mary of Magdala begun on Good Friday (see p. 103).

It has to be said that we do not know much about Mary of Magdala. It is implied, more than implied, that she was a woman of easy virtue. Certainly she is the only woman in the passion narratives who is defined solely by the place she came from – Magdala. Most of the other women, as was the custom of the time, are described in relation to their husbands or sons. So we read in the last chapters of all four gospels about:

- *Mary, mother of Jesus.*
- *The mother of the sons of Zebedee (she is nameless but is defined as Zebedee's wife and mother of two sons).*
- *Mary, mother of the younger James and Joseph.*
- *Salome and Joanna – both are named as though we should know them.*

> - *Mary, wife of Cleopas.*
> - *Mary from Magdala, the only woman at the time of death named in all four gospels.*
>
> *What was she like? Let's try to get inside the heart and mind of this striking and passionate woman.*

I had stayed with him on that Friday. With some of the other women, we followed. It was hard, but I had been certain, absolutely certain that God wouldn't let it happen. I had been so sure that there would be a splendid miracle at the last moment. But it hadn't come. And when I watched that dear man choke to death with the blood and water gurgling in his lungs I couldn't believe that it was happening. I hated God then. I could have killed him. How could he let Jesus down?

This wealthy man, Joseph someone called him, was given permission to take Jesus from the place of execution. I and some of the other women followed. I was terrified that something awful was going to happen to the body. But this man turned out to be all right; he had good intentions, and he put that dear broken body into a brand new grave. We noted the place precisely because we intended to return and do the right thing by Jesus – clean him and lay him out properly. Yes, we saw exactly where he was and we planned to go as soon as the Sabbath was over.

God. You can keep him. I'll never believe again. Jesus was the only one who has ever loved me. If God can do this to him . . . I hate him. But I'll be there on Sunday morning. As soon as the sun is up, I'll be there. Jesus can count on me.

When I got back to the lodgings, I thought I wouldn't sleep, but oddly enough, I did. I was shattered by the events and I slept for four or five hours almost as though I'd been drugged. Then I woke to the pain. The Sabbath dragged out. The others kept a low profile. Well, I don't blame them.

So I spent the day thinking. Jesus was the only man, the only person, who had ever loved me unconditionally. I did not know how I could live without him. And I still hated God. Or rather I felt he had died when Jesus had. There was nothing left.

Straight away after sundown and the ending of the Sabbath, I was out at the bazaar in a flash to buy some of the best burial spices and ointments. That night I packed my basket and arranged with two of the others to get up early. It was that night I couldn't sleep. And when I got up at the back of four o'clock on the morning of the first day of the week I felt a wreck.

However, this was something I knew I had to do. So the three of us, Salome and Mary, the mother of young James, and I, set off. We didn't speak much but we were worried about the weight of the stone. What if we couldn't move it? Even with the three of us? But we hurried along as quietly as possible. It was still dark when we left but the sun rose just as we arrived. It was going to be a scorcher today. The ground was wet with dew and we went straight to the place. We had all taken particular note of it and there was no argy-bargy. We went straight to the spot. But as we got closer, we saw that the stone had been rolled back. We got nearer. There was something going on inside the cave and when we looked in there was a young man there, a young man in white. I was scared out of my wits.

'He's not here,' he said. We looked wildly round thinking we'd made a mistake. 'This is the place,' he said. 'Go and tell the disciples that he will meet them in Galilee.' We stumbled out and ran to the edge of the cemetery and then stopped. Had he not been really dead? Had he managed to escape? A wild hope seized me. But then reason took over. He had been dead all right. I know a dead body when I see one. Besides they were going to break his legs to hasten the death and they saw that he was already dead. *They* certified the death. And then terror took over and we ran and ran. What was going on? We never spoke to each other far less anyone else. Then I thought of all those expensive spices. I had left them there in my basket. Cost a bomb they had. And it was the right tomb. And there *had* been someone there.

They've laughed at me often before. Once more will make no difference. Then I go back to the old life. So I went to see Simon Peter, who was lodging with Mary and John. I never said anything about young men and messages. I've always known when to keep my mouth shut. But I told him that the body had gone.

Well, the two of them were off like a shot and I struggled to keep up. John was there first and then Peter arrived all out of breath, ducked his head and went inside. He came out and shook his head and the pair of them went back home. They never spoke to me of course.

Then it hit me. He had died and had gone. For the others, life would just go on. For me, everything had been taken away. I started to cry. Not nice genteel tears. I put my head against the wall and bawled. I couldn't get enough air into my lungs for the crying I had to do. Was it my fault that he had died? Was it because of us he had been crucified? And where was God? Then I felt someone was near. I tried to stop and wiped my face with my skirt. Through the haze of my tears I saw a groundsman or a gardener.

'Why are you crying? Who are you looking for?' he asked.

'They've taken him away.' I tried to speak calmly but my voice had big cracks in it and my throat was sore. 'Can you help? Do you know where he is?' A wild hope began then. Maybe after all I would see his dead body. Then the gardener spoke in a voice I knew. 'Mary!' God in heaven it was himself. 'Master?' I said.

'Jesus? Jesus? It is you. It is!' And I laughed and cried and tried to hug him. He smiled in that wonderful way and said, 'Now, Mary, this must be shared. Go and tell them. Go and tell those brothers of mine that I am going to be with my God and your God for ever.'

I stood back and stared at him. He raised his hand as a farewell and smiled. And I ran, again, and hammered at the door. They wouldn't answer and I went on hammering. Later I realised they had thought it was the authorities. Eventually the door opened a small crack. And I put my hand in so that they wouldn't close it.

'I've seen him.'

'Who?'

Sweet Jesus! How can they be so stupid? I began again.

'I've seen him. I have seen the Lord. I have seen Jesus of Nazareth. I have spoken to him today. Just now in the garden.'

They pulled me in to the house after that and quizzed me about what had happened. So I told them again. But it was as though terror had taken hold of them and they did nothing – nothing!

I went back to my lodgings after that. My mind, my soul, my spirit, my body, my whole being was flooded with light. God was alive again with me and in me. I knew then that Jesus would somehow make himself known to those lovely, stupid, self-important men. Jesus would make it right.

And for me? I didn't know what the future would be. But one thing I did know. I would not be going back to the old life. Jesus would not let me. I washed and put on clean clothes and braided my hair. And I ate some bread with Salome and Mary, mother of young James. I told them and we talked about it. Bless them, they believed me.

I went outside and walked. I walked in the souk, the market place. I went near the Temple. I went outside the city and saw the place where they had killed him. Then I climbed up to the garden on the Mount of Olives where they had arrested him. I had blamed the men after that. But now I think it may have been part of a plan – of Jesus or of God. Every place seemed hallowed and beautiful. He was alive. For me, life had changed for ever. This new step, this new living Jesus would be part of our life with him. We would have to share it; Jesus was always on about sharing – bread, money, water, wine, good news – we would share it with the folk in Galilee, with the ones in Judea. Perhaps with everyone. And we would do it together. Jesus would tell us. Jesus would show us. We would share it with everyone.

And I would change. It would be impossible now to go back. With this new hidden strength and presence I would begin a new life. I, who had never had a stable family, might even be given one by Jesus. I, who had been despised by men, shunned by women and feared by children, may be given, would be given a new life. Jesus would show me.

Serene and confident I stood and looked at the city in the midday sun. I heard a child's voice. 'Amma,' it said. Amma, Mother. 'Amma. I'm lost.' I had never seen him before. He looked up at me full of trust and put his hand in mine and we walked down the hill to find his family. Dear God, I thought, life has changed for everyone, everywhere, till the end of time.

18

Fear and Silence

EASTER[1]

Readings:	Isaiah 25:6–9
	1 Corinthians 1–11
	Mark 16:1–8
Season:	Easter Day

'They said nothing to anyone for they were afraid' (Mark 16:8).

I like a good ending to a story. It need not be a happy ending, although that is very nice. But it has to be a satisfactory ending.

When we read in Charlotte Brontë's *Jane Eyre*, 'Reader, I married him,' we all sigh with relief, although most of us saw it coming from the moment Jane Eyre and Mr Rochester met. Did you watch *Pride and Prejudice* on television? Mr Darcy and Miss Eliza Bennet were certainly going to get together. They were an item from the start, although they did not recognise it. Possibly most of those who watched the production had read the book anyway. But we watched six enthralling hour-long episodes to see it all.

In a good whodunit, the ending has to be rounded off, finished, satisfactory. Not just 'who-*dun*-it', but how, and why, and what the clues were. Dorothy Sayers' *The Nine Tailors* is a classic, with the bells of the church, the nine tailors of the title, weaving the pattern through the book and supplying the ending. Or take

Knowledge of Angels by Jill Paton Walsh, a classic statement against fundamentalism of all sorts, with magnificent suspense holding the reader to the last page – a most enthralling ending. Yes, whether a love story, a crime story or a modern novel, a satisfactory ending is essential.

And in Mark's gospel we have the most famous event in the world told with a very *un*satisfactory ending. 'They said nothing to anybody for they were afraid.' Lorimer in the Scots Bible translates: 'An they tauld naebodie naething, sae afeared war they.' And there it just ends.

This appears to be the original ending of the gospel. Perhaps there was another ending which became torn or damaged. Certainly the verses from verse 16 onwards were cobbled together much later in an attempt, or more than one attempt, to round the book off. Can the writer of the first gospel really have left us with no resurrection appearance? Just the empty tomb? Maybe he did plan something more, but this is what we have. 'They said nothing to anyone for they were afraid.' I find these among the most movingly authentic verses of the whole Bible.

Let's try to relive that Friday and Saturday. We know that the men who had followed the Galilean had run away, with the exception of John, and perhaps John Mark, a young lad, a teenager perhaps, who just possibly is the Mark of Mark's gospel. It was cowardly, but *very* understandable. I think the men were much more likely to be arrested than the women. It was expected that the women would be there for rites of birth and death. So, of course, there they were. But listen to the roll call. By Jewish standards of the day, it is quite remarkable.

- Mark says many women from Galilee were there and also some from Jerusalem. He names three, Mary, another Mary, mother of James and Joses, and a woman called Salome.

- Matthew writes of many women and specifically names Mary Magdalene, Mary the mother of James and Joseph, and the mother of the sons of Zebedee.

- Luke mentions the women from Galilee. But they are only named when he tells of the resurrection. Then he names them as Mary of Magdala, Joanna, Mary the mother of James, and other women.

- John writes of Mary, the mother of Jesus, and her sister, also an unnamed woman who is the wife of Cleopas, and Mary Magdalene.

After the death, Joseph of Arimathaea bravely asked Pilate for the body. When permission was granted, Joseph bought a new linen cloth (not a cheap article) and wrapped Jesus up in it. He put him in a tomb cut out of rock and a stone was rolled against the entrance. And, we are told, the two Marys were watching. The last verse of chapter 15 is clear:

> And Mary of Magdala and Mary the mother of Joseph were watching and saw where Jesus was laid.

So those two women plus their friend Salome *knew* where the body of Jesus was. When they arrived two days' later, very early on the Sunday morning, they *knew* where to go. They came with the oils that were necessary for the embalming and laying out. Probably they were worn out from crying and disappointment.

It's bad enough when a really elderly person dies, or someone who has had a long painful and wasting illness. But when someone young, just thirty or so, dies then the grief is sharper and angrier. But Jesus didn't just die. He was executed horribly and cruelly. And not only did he not deserve to die, but he had been good and loving, and, as far as these women were concerned, he had been a gift from God for them – a very special person. So it wasn't even an ordinary grief, if ever grief can be said to be ordinary. It was a grief racked with disappointment and sorrow for the lost cause and the vision that had crashed around them. So it was all over. And he was just one more fine young man who had died. A hero, in his way, but a dead hero.

I don't think they were expecting anything except the peculiar comfort of being busy in doing the best that could be done for the person who had died. For there *is* a strange comfort in doing your very best for someone you love who has died. They would have the best of oils for Jesus, and the best spices that they could afford. And how they would be glad to wash clean the wounded and dirty body. And then they came to that yawning empty tomb. They bent over and went inside the tomb and found a young man who told them that Jesus had been raised from the dead and the disciples and Peter would see him again in Galilee. To find the stone rolled away was worrying. To find the tomb empty must have been alarming. But to find a strange youth giving such a message must have been plain terrifying.

> So they went out and fled from the tomb, for terror and amazement had seized them; and they said nothing to anyone, for they were afraid.

That verse, full of terror and silence, running away and cowardice, is for me an authentic resurrection verse. It assures me of a reality by its honesty and openness. This is no fairy story. This verse is a signpost pointing to the truth, and pointing me to faith. There were no heroes at the cross. And now at the empty tomb there are no heroines. If Mark and the others had been making the story up, they would have had triumphal assertions and victory drums and speeches of vindication. Mark ends his gospel with the stark words of human failure, 'and they said nothing to anyone, for they were afraid'.

The resurrection, whether then or now, is not something that is blindingly obvious. It is not something that has compelling logic about it. It is not a doctrine that is self-evident to people who read the accounts. Nor was it (and this is the surprising thing), self-evident to the people who were the first witnesses of the resurrection. According to Mark, the first people were so frightened they didn't tell *anyone* what they had seen and heard.

When we have an experience that goes deep, we don't rush around talking about it. We cherish it. We reflect upon it. We hold it within to see if it is real. I think more people than we realise have had experiences that go deep, intensely personal experiences, perhaps unexpected. Maybe they are difficult to talk about. But often there is a sense of that which is more than this world, something breaking through and tapping us on the shoulder. And if this happens to us we do not rush around telling about it, in case we are laughed at. We may choose not to talk about it in case people, by their questions, take away the precious moment we want to hold on to.

The Easter experience celebrated by the church is full of singing and joy and affirmation. And that is good and right. But the authentic Easter experience for most of us is I believe much nearer to the experience of those women – tentative, puzzling, partial, personal – and when it comes to us we tell nobody at first because we are frightened.

The resurrection doesn't solve all the problems of life. I know people still ask questions and have problems. That's all right. Jesus doesn't ask us to understand, he asks us to follow. There is still a step of faith. The women that first Easter morning were too scared to take it in. But later they did.

The resurrection with all its implications *is* frightening. What possibilities there are now! In what surprising places the Risen Christ may yet meet you and me, calling us to newness of life.

And he does, oh he does! Life is literally open-ended. No wonder the women ran away and said nothing. They were afraid, afraid of all the terrifying and glorious opportunities and responsibilities, and so perhaps are we, today, afraid. For Christ is risen! He is risen indeed. Hallelujah!

NOTE

1. This sermon was preached at Toorak Uniting Church, Melbourne, Easter Day, 1999.

19

Padlocks and Prayer

ASCENSION

Readings:	Acts 1:6–14
	Ephesians 1:15–23
	Luke 24:44–53
Season:	Ascension Sunday

Have you ever had a time in your life when you appeared to be living in a dream of some sort?

It may have been a wonderful time, perhaps connected with falling in love and being married. Perhaps it was when you moved to deeper love and commitment and planned to start a family. Or for you it may have been a fabulous new job or an amazing holiday. Perhaps it was a cruise, a tour abroad, something that was so special that for ever afterwards you thought of life before . . . and life afterwards.

Of course the defining moment for you may have been one of deep sadness, connected with illness or failing health. Perhaps it was the death of a dearly loved person. And for ever afterwards there was a defining time of before . . . or afterwards. In both cases, the event or series of events may at the time have had a dreamlike quality about them. As though it were real, but you were also standing outside yourself and watching yourself as well.

The event we celebrated at Easter must have been one of those times. Jesus had died. There was no possible doubt about it. There was blood and a body. There was a grave and a tomb and a seal and a guard upon the tomb. He was dead. Then on the Sunday the tomb was wide open. There wasn't a body. But there were appearances where Jesus undoubtedly came and spoke and ate and talked to his friends. Then just as disconcertingly he would go away again. The appearances were in Jerusalem, then they stopped so the disciples trooped home to Galilee (presumably splitting up the group at that point), but he followed them to Galilee and started showing up on the shore and having baked fish breakfasts with some of them. He wasn't there when they needed him, but he kept showing up just as they had decided he had gone. It was a most disconcerting time, even an unsatisfactory time. During that time, what were they thinking? Did they want him back for good? Or was there something going on that was very embarrassing and difficult? What, for example, did Peter tell his wife?

> Jesus has been crucified and he's dead, and so I've come back home to help with the family fishing business, but Jesus came to see us this morning, and no, he won't come home this time like he used to, because he says he's going back to Jerusalem, at least we think that's what he was on about. And, no, I actually don't know where he is at the moment. But I have to look after his sheep.

It sounds pretty lame stuff if you ask me. So I believe that there was an air of dreaming about the whole thing. Sometimes he was hauntingly real in their minds even when he was not physically present. Sometimes he *was* literally present and they were full of pent-up confusion and questions and love and even anger. And then he was away again.

And then forty days after the resurrection, there was, according to Luke, a final goodbye. Mind you, it has to be said that the others don't mention it as an event. The first time Luke tells us about it, it is almost as though it happened that first Easter evening. But very soon it became known and believed in the early church. The event has always been known as the ascension, the going up. It is the official end of Easter. The paschal candle is taken away, the Easter egg tree is finally dismantled. Easter is over for another year. But what is the ascension? What is this Going Up?

At Christmas, God came to be in the human baby born in Bethlehem. At the ascension, the humanity of Jesus is taken to be with God. The whole history of the world changed when Jesus was born. And at the ascension, we perceive a change in God. As Jesus is in God, so now is our humanity in God. God knows about our suffering and weakness. And the ascension, the going up, proclaims to us and to all believers that Jesus is enthroned. And so we sing songs like 'The head that once was crowned with thorns is crowned with glory now'. Or 'Crown him with many crowns, the lamb upon the throne'.

But let's go back to the disciples in the *dwam-like*[1] state they were in. Finally, he had gone. There was no doubt about it this time. He had finally and irrevocably said 'Goodbye'. There would be no more dropping in for bread and wine at supper with Mr and Mrs Cleopas. There would be no more fish breakfasts on the shore. There would be no more enigmatic conversations about feeding sheep. He had finally gone. But it was *still* not over. Although they may have been uncertain before, they appeared now to have accepted certain things. He had died. He had risen. He had appeared several times. He had gone for good to be with God. And he had promised something. So the big question was 'How do we live now?' 'What do we do now?' They were living on the edge of a volcano, only they didn't know where the volcano was or when it would erupt. So they did what the church has always been good at doing – praying behind locked doors.

The picture on the order of service this morning is of Jesus with his arms stretching beyond the edges of the world, beyond sun and moon and stars, and telling his friends that he would be with them always. And the picture on the back of the order makes me laugh. There they all are, packed in an upper room, praying like mad, behind locked doors. A very large padlock is there to show how securely locked they were. It makes me laugh because Jesus has another trick up his sleeve. *We* know what it is. Jesus lets them pray for a week more, then he unleashes the Holy Spirit. The doors are flung open and those poor scared fishermen and housewives and tax collectors and prostitutes and goodness knows who else must face the world with their unbelievable and amazing and heart-arresting stories. He is alive. His cross stands empty to the skies. He is gloriously among us. He has been crowned in heaven and God weeps with our grief and pain.

God weeps for the Kosovan refugees. God weeps for the evil of Milosovic. God weeps for the men who drop the bombs and for the men or man who makes the decisions. And Christ in majesty walks the roads of Serbia and Edinburgh, daring us to leave our everyday life and to follow.

- To follow with no guarantee of success.
- To follow with no guarantee of reward.
- To follow with no guarantee of comfort.

But Christ in majesty challenges us to live in a Christ-like way. None of us manages to do it for very long. Occasionally it happens, and the knowledge is intimate and sweet. But most of the time we muddle along behind securely padlocked doors, either in the church, or at work, or at home. Or else the padlock is on our role, our personality, what we have always been or thought or done, and we cannot bear to change because that would be too painful, so let's keep the padlock on. Padlocks and prayer; that should be pretty safe. But it's not.

At Pentecost, God broke the padlocks and unleashed the Holy Spirit. And probably the rushing sound we shall read about next week was Jesus laughing around earth and heaven. This week, as a preparation for Pentecost, let us look at those padlocks. Let us see what our fears may be or our barriers to growth.

- Is it rampant sectarianism?
- Is it fear of Judaism or Islam or other religions?
- Is it fear of being laughed at or ridiculed?
- Is it homophobia?
- Is it something from the past that has us in a vice?
- Is it someone we cannot forgive?
- Is it something we know we should do but are too timid or proud?

What will the Holy Spirit have in store for us when we have stopped praying behind locked doors? What will the Holy Spirit say to you and to me when the padlocks are broken and God's glorious power breaks upon us at Pentecost?

NOTE

1. *Dwam* in Scots means dream or reverie.

20

The Barking Pig

PENTECOST

Readings:	*Numbers 11:24–30*
	Acts 2:1–21
	John 20:19–23
Season:	*Pentecost*

I want to tell you three stories – two of which we have already read today.

First, here is a true story told by a friend, David McBriar,[1] who is a Franciscan friar in North Carolina. It is about a Primary One teacher who had to produce some sort of pageant or show which involved *everyone* in her class of five-year-olds – even the shy ones, and the ones who couldn't learn lines, and the bossy ones, and the charming ones, and the downright difficult ones. She had one of those! He was called Norman.

She decided to do *Cinderella*. There would be parts for everyone. There were the plum parts for pretty, clever children, there were fun parts for the natural comics, there were loads of walk-on parts for the shy children, like mice and rats and footmen and courtiers and servants, not to mention the pumpkin.

All the children had parts that they wanted except one – Norman.

'Norman, what are you going to be?' asked the teacher.

'I'm going to be the pig.'

'Pig? There's no pig in Cinderella.'

'Well, there is now.'

And, like the good teacher she was, she drafted in a pig to the script and let Norman organise his own costume. And he did. Flesh-coloured leggings, a pink T-shirt, a curly pipe-cleaner for a tail and a paper cup for his nose, Norman was Pig. Ignoring the part specially written for him, he became Cinderella's presence. He ambled along on all fours beside her. He sat back on his haunches and observed what was going on. He would express on his face whatever was happening at the moment. He became the commentary on the play. In case you were in any doubt about what was happening, you could look at Norman, and there you could see, at different moments of the play:

- sadness
- anger
- worry
- amazement
- anxiety
- hope
- distress
- disappointment
- hope
- exhilaration

Norman was there! At the climax of the play, when the prince finally placed the slipper on the tiny foot of Cinderella, Norman went wild with joy. He pranced around on his hind legs and finally began to bark like a dog. At the curtain call Norman, the barking pig, received a standing ovation. Of course Prince Charming and

Cinderella were well clapped, but the two undoubted heroes were a barking pig and an exhausted teacher.

Now let's get back to the story we read, a story standing on the edge of history – from the book of Numbers.

Moses took seventy of the elders and brought them round the Tent of the meeting, that holy place where God could be worshipped. And the writer tells us that Moses had received a measure of spirit – a finite amount, a measured portion (not a limitless reservoir, but a set proportion). So for the elders to get some, God had to take away some of what had already been given to Moses. And that amount was divided into seventy and given to the elders. Two had got left behind in the camp – I wonder if that was the senior elder and one of the younger ones staying behind to help him with his zimmer? Anyway, although they weren't there, they got the spirit too – and fell into an ecstasy and began to prophesy. Joshua was worried and made a formal complaint: here are these two elders behaving in a disorderly fashion. They must be disciplined. And Moses said, 'I wish all the Lord's people were prophets, and that the Lord would send his spirit on all of them!'

The third story is the well-known Pentecost account. I imagine that the apostles with the extra man, Matthias, to replace Judas, were an extremely nervous bunch. What on earth was going to happen next? They tried to be orderly. They obviously felt that twelve was the correct number. They were trying, I think, to control things and help them to happen in a decent and orderly fashion.

Remember, they didn't have even the normal comfort of a death. And those words are not intended in any way to minimise the pain and shock of a death. But they didn't have a body. They had resurrection appearances and *dis*appearances. And now he said he was going for good – but could you believe it? He had also said that he would come again – was this it? The end of the world?

And then he said he would send his spirit – would it be *his* spirit, divided into twelve and parcelled out among the apostles? What was going through their minds? One thing was certain. They would gather and pray. That had to be right. Then came the noise like wind. Then there were flames of fire. Then came the miraculous speaking in tongues – not crazy unknown language, but good real languages so that all the foreigners who had come to Jerusalem for the feast of Pentecost could understand what was being said. And *then* for my money the real miracle happens. When people say, 'What's happening?', Peter gets up and preaches to them.

Peter, *Peter*, that craven, pushy, denying, bossy fisherman, gets up and preaches to them. And three thousand, *three thousand*, were converted. And you bet the apostles didn't know what to do.

This blessing of God could not be handled. It was beyond all expectation.

Recently I heard of a formal service held in one of our cathedrals. One of the hymns used came out on the order of service with a misprint in the first line. Instead of, 'There's a wideness in God's mercy', there was printed, 'There's a *wildness* in God's mercy'. But there is. There *is* a wildness in God's mercy. Not just the twelve apostles to have the spirit – but three thousand total strangers. Not just the Jews to receive God's mercy, but the gentiles and non-Jews. Not just the people of Palestine to receive the gospel, but the people of Scotland and all over the world. And not just the natural leaders and religious folk to be given the gift, but fishermen and tax-gatherers, joiners and prostitutes, housewives and civil servants. There's a wildness in God's mercy.

And that takes us back to Norman, the barking pig. It is not just the charming princes nor the pretty heroines who are centre stage in God's production. It may be the elders of Moses who didn't get to the right place at the right time who are suddenly centre stage. It may be startled first-century Egyptian Jews who are centre stage. It is not just the high flyers and intellectually able who receive the Spirit and are called to spread the gospel. It is especially the weak and the vulnerable, who can see what is happening and interpret it to the others.

One Christmas Day, in our home, at about 4 p.m., with three large services taken in the previous twenty-four hours and a Christmas dinner for fourteen family and overseas students behind me, I was in the kitchen emptying the dishwasher and setting out the Christmas cake for tea. The door opened and in walked Lesley, aged thirty-something in physical years, but with learning difficulties making her possibly about three or four in mental age. She had left the games and laughter in the sitting-room to search me out. The conversation went something like this:

Question: 'What you doing?' Answer: 'I'm clearing up.'

Question: 'What you doing?' Answer: 'I'm emptying the dish-washer.'

Question: 'What you doing?' Answer: 'I'm setting the tray for tea.'

Question: 'What you doing?'

Clearly no answer satisfied her. I wasn't able to ask the right question and she was not able to articulate what was in her heart, so I said, 'Lesley, what do *you* think I'm doing?'

She looked at me for a few seconds, then, with a huge effort, took my sleeve and began to lead me out of the kitchen. 'You work too hard,' she said. All the people in the sitting-room playing games had not noticed that I had slipped out to tidy up. It was the woman with learning difficulties who had the seeing eye and the heart to question. It is indeed not just the high flyers and intellectually able who receive the Spirit.

- It may be the person racked by grief who is best able to show love and sympathy.

- It may be the man with depression who is best able to recognise pain in another.
- It may be a child who asks the searching question.
- It may be the woman with learning difficulties who can see most clearly.
- It may be people who feel within that they have failed who know most about how to live.

It may be the church in the poorest countries of the world, working against an intolerable background of poverty who are centre stage. It may be the children of this church saving money for a well in Malawi. Or it may be you, sitting quietly in your pew on a Sunday morning. God wants, needs, all of us, to take part in the Pentecost experience. Maybe today, God calls you to be a barking pig. God *certainly* pours out the Holy Spirit upon you.

NOTE

1. David J. McBriar, O.F.M., *Love in a Paper Sack* (Raleigh, North Carolina: published privately, 1995), p. 82.